Fergus Ontario in Colour Photos, Saving Our History One Photo at a Time

Photography
by Barbara Raue
updated 2016

Series Name:
Cruising Ontario

Book 68: Fergus

Cover photo: Gothic Revival house, Page 45

Series Name: Cruising Ontario
Saving Our History One Photo at a Time

Series Name: Cruising Ontario
Saving Our History One Photo at a Time

Book 120-121: Amherstburg
Book 122: Essex
Book 123-124: Kingsville
Book 125-127: Woodstock
Book 128: Thamesford
Book 129-132: St. Marys
Book 133-136: Sarnia
Book 137-138: Welland
Book 139-144: Kingston

Other Books by Barbara Raue

Coins of Gold –biography of May Todd

Arrows, Indians and Love – historical fiction

The Life and Times of Barbara
Volume 1: Inventions That Have Enhanced My Life
Volume 2: Entertainment That I Have Enjoyed
Volume 3: East Coast Trips
Volume 4: Olympics Have Always Intrigued Me
Volume 5: Wonders of the World
Volume 6: Caribbean Cruises We Have Enjoyed
Volume 7: Animals
Volume 8: Storms and Other Major Disasters in My Lifetime
Volume 9: Wars, Terrorist Attacks and Major Disasters

The Cromwell Family Book

Laura Secord Discovered – historical fiction

Daddy Where Are You? - Memoir

Visit Barbara's website to view all of her books
http://barbararaue.ca

Fergus

Fergus is the largest community in Centre Wellington, a township within Wellington County. It lies on the Grand River about 25 kilometers north of Guelph.

The first settlers to this area were freed slaves who formed what was known as the Pierpoint Settlement, named after their leader, Richard Pierpoint. Along with half a dozen other men, Pierpoint was granted land in Garafraxa Township in what is now Fergus.

Adam Fergusson visited Canada in 1831 to investigate emigration for the Highland Society of Scotland. In 1833 in partnership with a fellow Scot, James Webster, they purchased over 7,000 acres of uncleared land in Nichol Township. Attracted by the abundant water power, they laid out the town of Fergus. Webster took up residence there and supervised the settlement's early development. The first house was built in 1833, then a hotel, a saw mill, grist mill, church and school.

They established a vibrant economy using the waterfalls on the Grand River as power for local industry. The Scots built solid stone houses, factories and other buildings which have characterized Fergus to this day. Many of the houses and factories built by these early settlers are still in use today.

Originally Fergus was known as Little Falls, because of the scenic waterfalls downtown between the Public Library and the Fergus Market.

St Andrew Street runs parallel to the Grand River on the north side and is the heart of downtown. On the south side of the river is Queen Street where the newly renovated Fergus Market is located.

Table of Contents

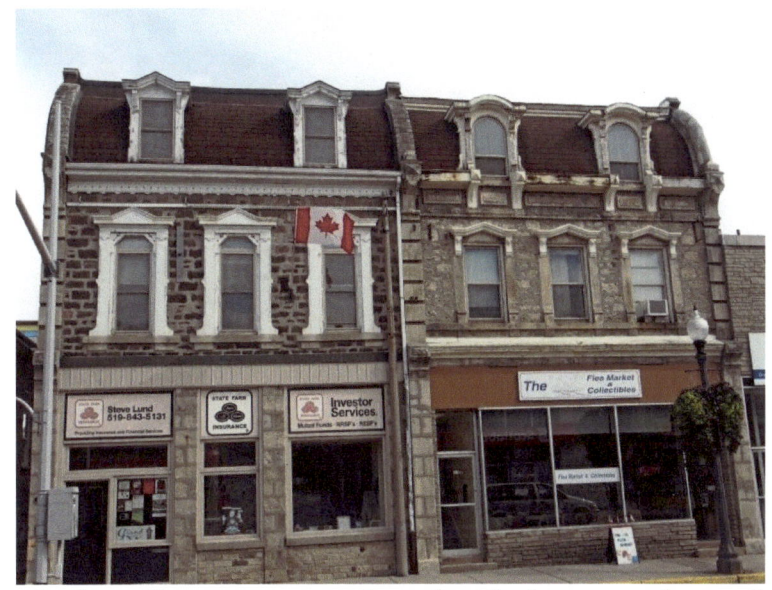

St. Andrew Street - mansard roof with dormers, decorative window hoods, cobblestone architecture

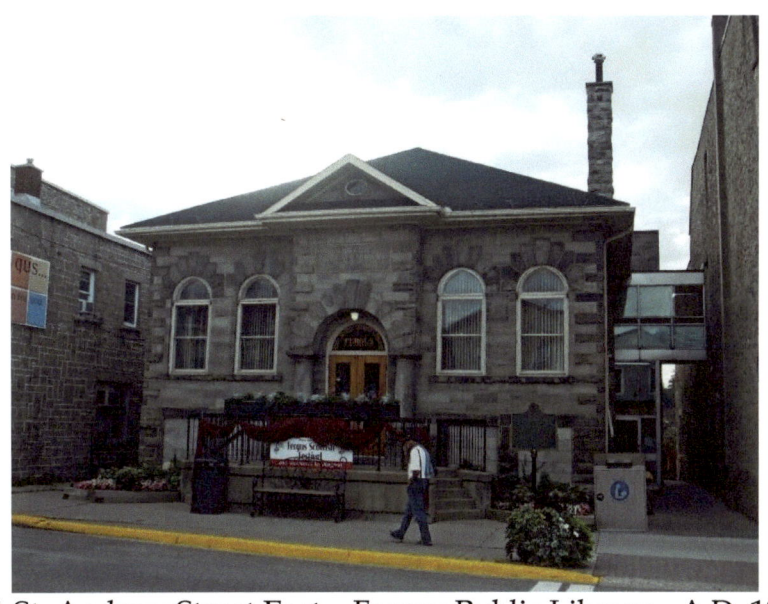

181 St. Andrew Street East – Fergus Public Library - A.D. 1910
Window voussoirs, Doric columns, pediment with circular window in tympanum

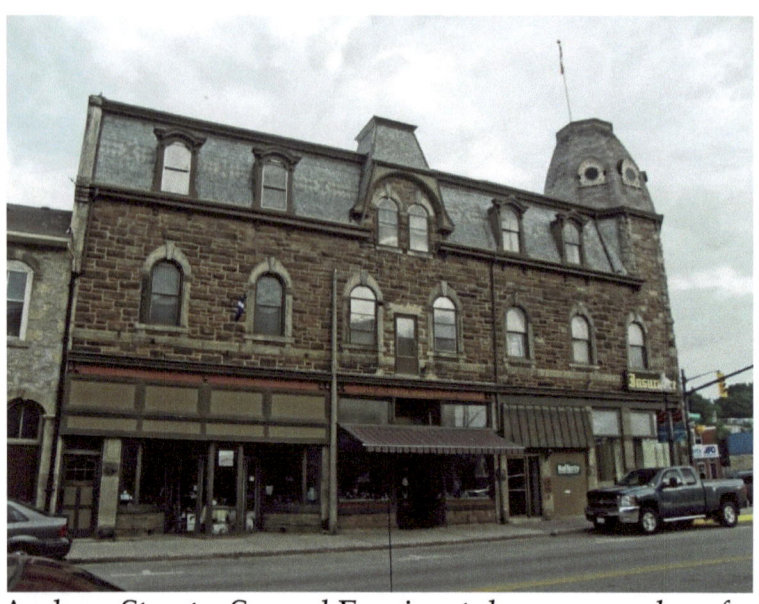

St. Andrew Street – Second Empire style – mansard roof with dormers, window hoods, arched window voussoirs and keystones

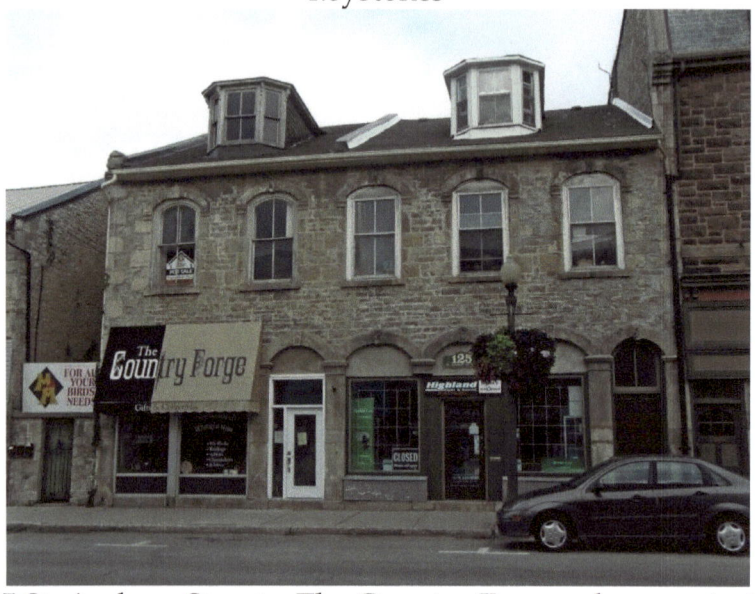

125 St. Andrew Street – The Country Forge - dormers in the attic, Doric columns surrounding doors

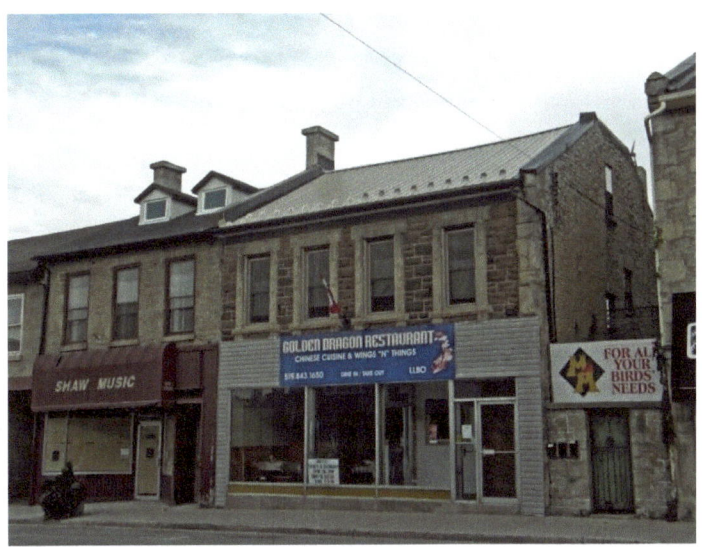

Limestone

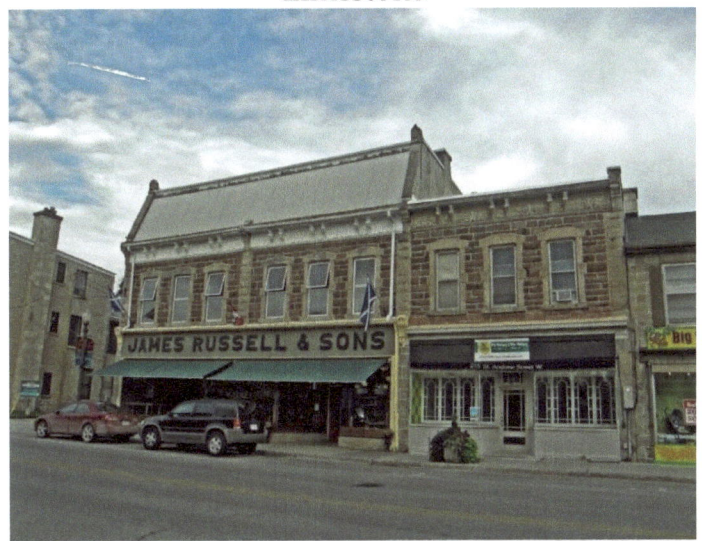

St. Andrew Street – James Russell & Sons Dry Goods store

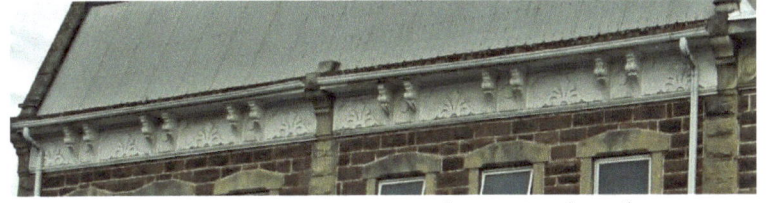

Decorative cornice, paired cornice brackets

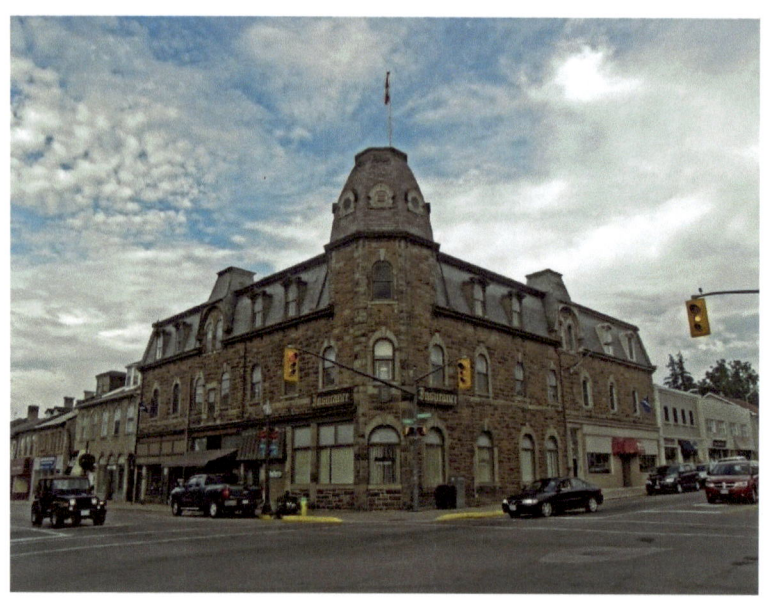

St. Andrew Street and St. David Street corner – Second Empire style – mansard roof with dormers, window hoods four-storey tower

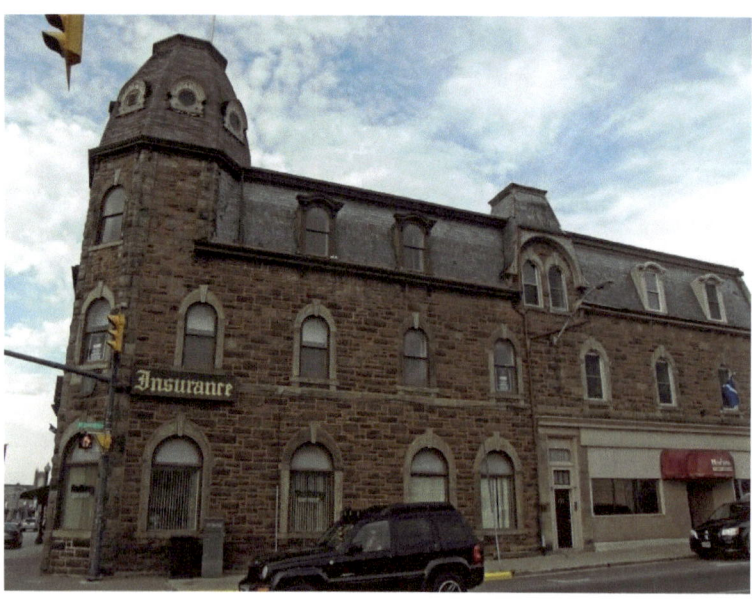

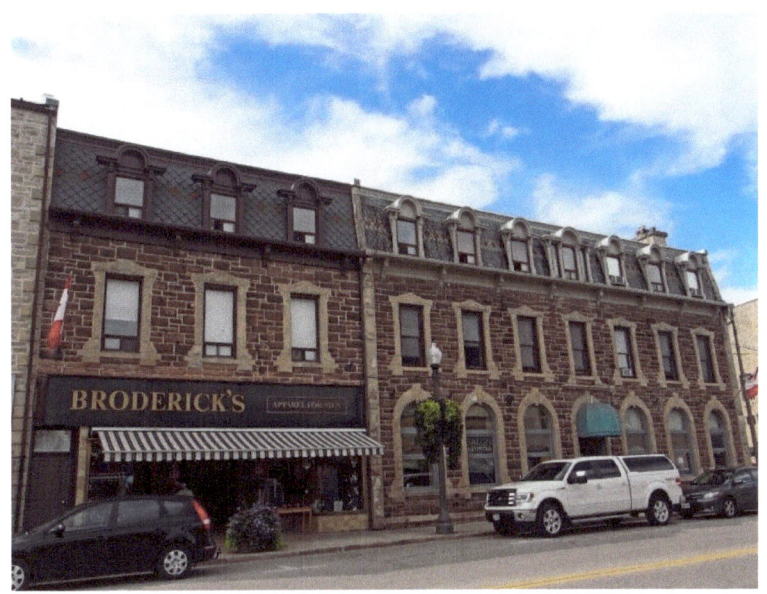

Second Empire style - window hoods on dormers in mansard roof, dichromatic tilework

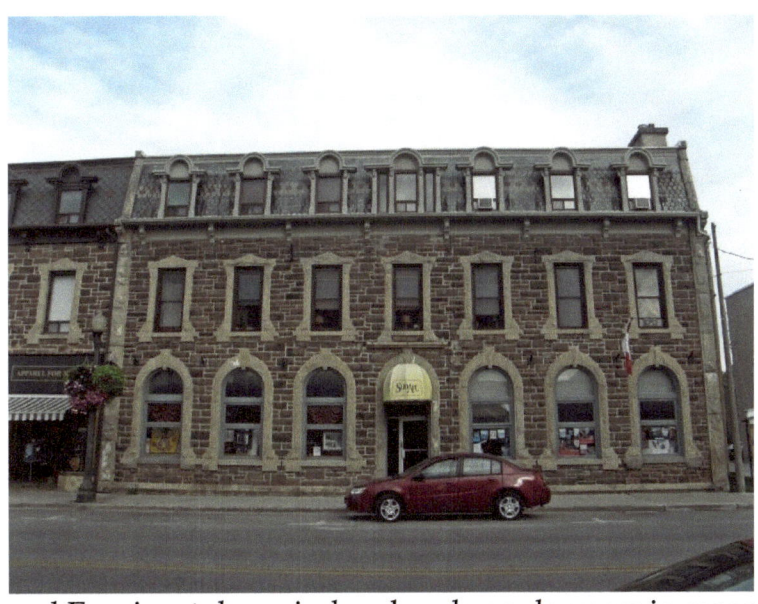

Second Empire style - window hoods on dormers in mansard roof, dichromatic tilework, arched window voussoirs with keystones on ground floor

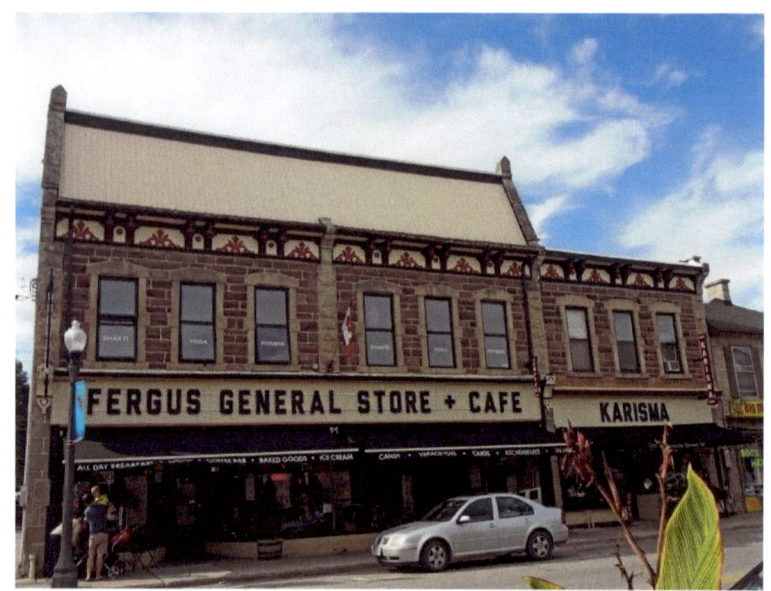

227-215 St. Andrew Street West – Fergus General Store & Café
- paired cornice brackets with decoration

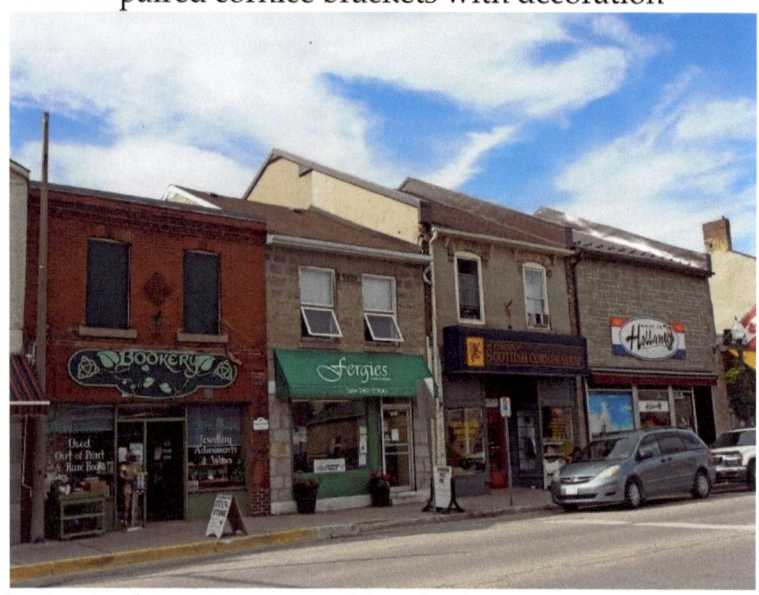

191 St. Andrew Street – red brick, dentil moulding; #187 –
Fergie's Fine Foods – limestone; #181 – Fergus Scottish Corner
Shop – cornice brackets, voussoirs

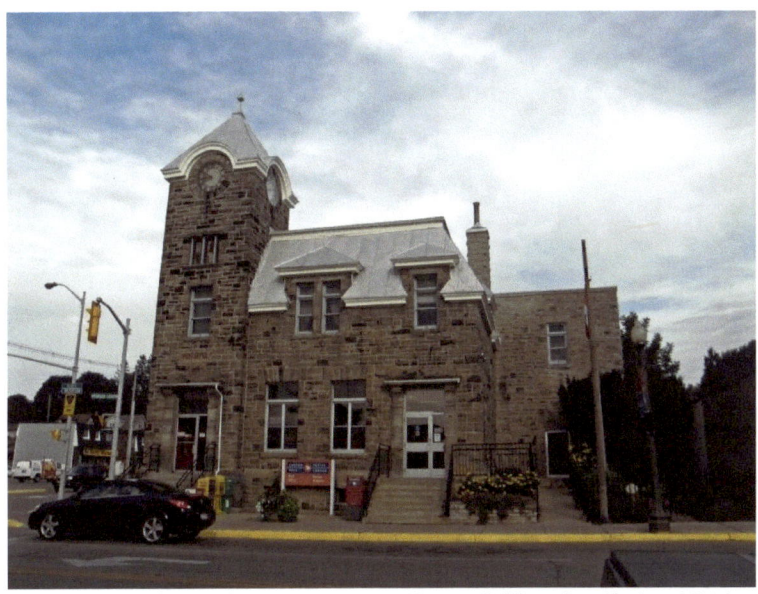

299 St. Andrew Street West - Post Office built in 1911 – stone building with clock tower, window hoods on second floor windows

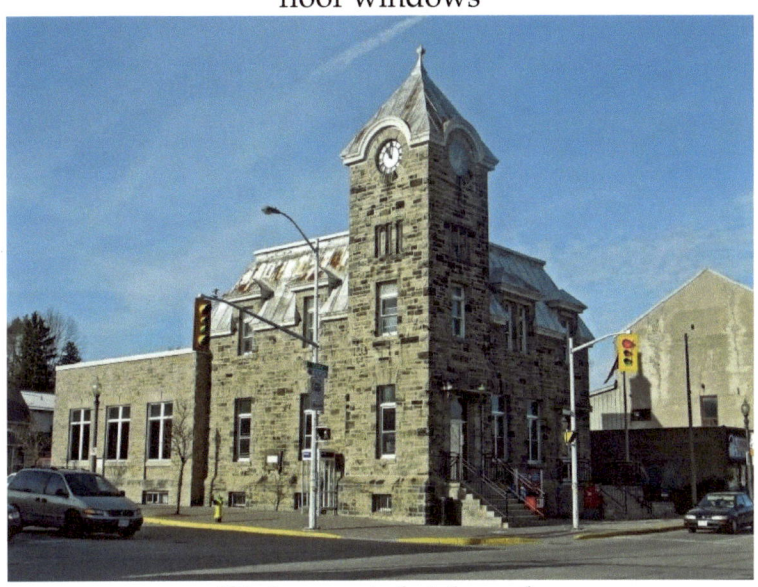

Dichromatic brickwork

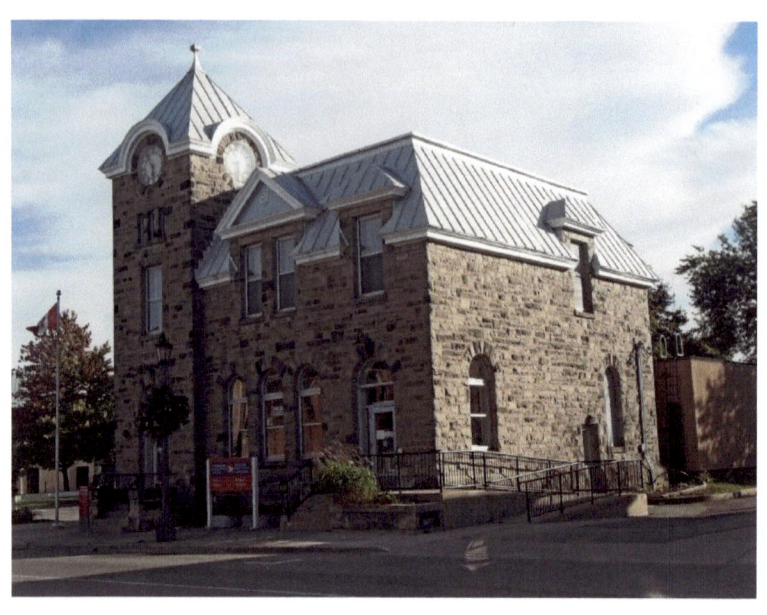

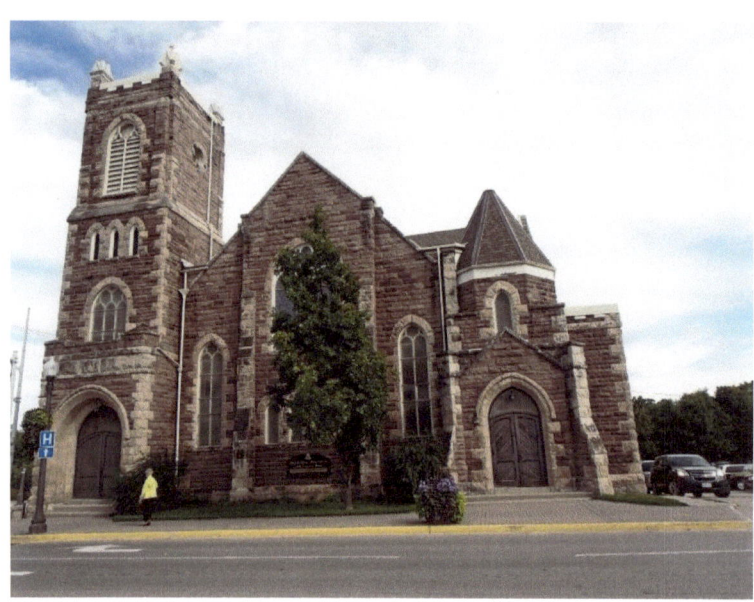

300 St. Andrew Street West - Melville United Church

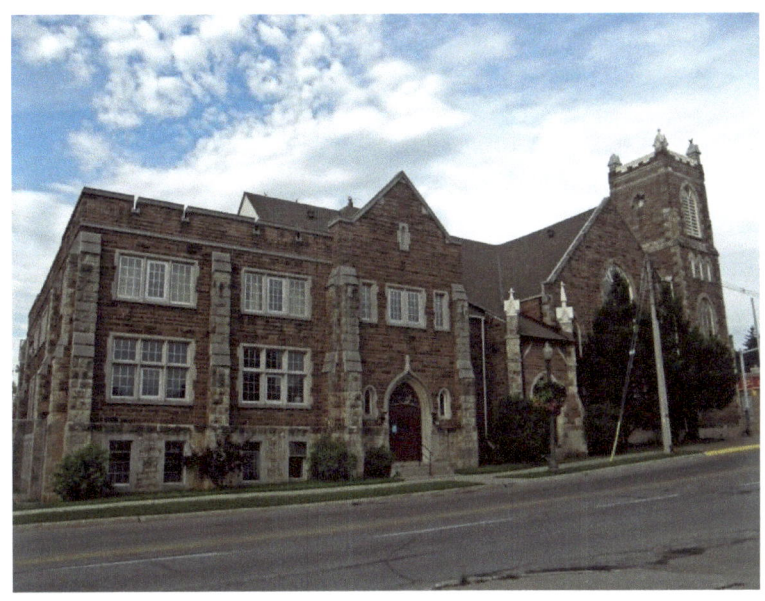

300 St. Andrew Street West - Melville United Church, Fergus
Buttresses, corner quoins

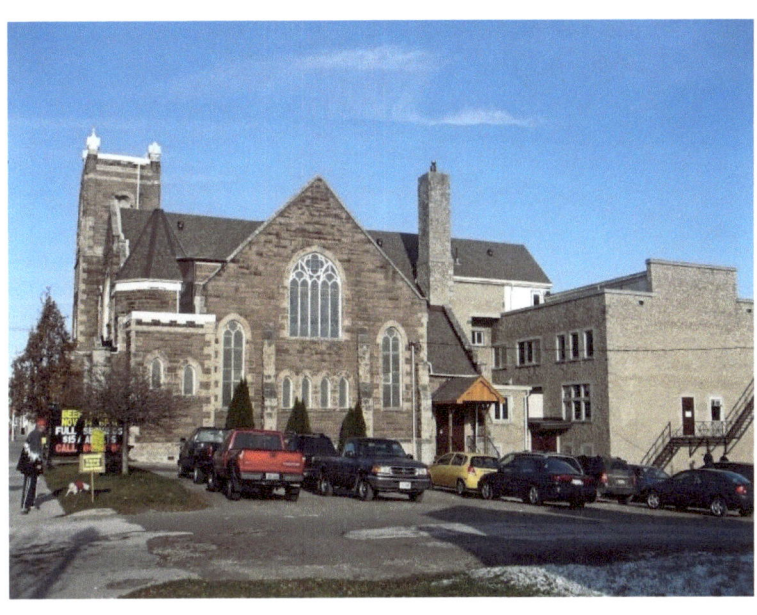

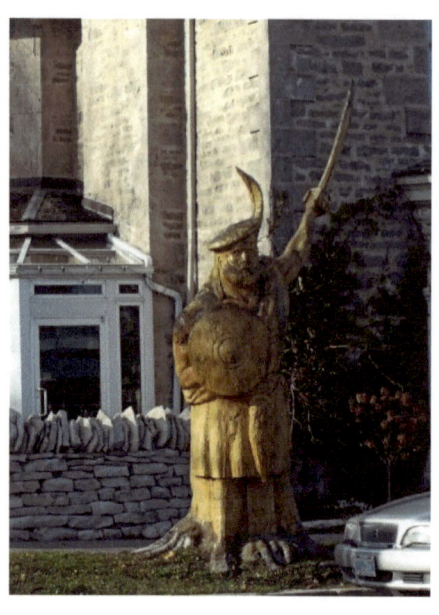

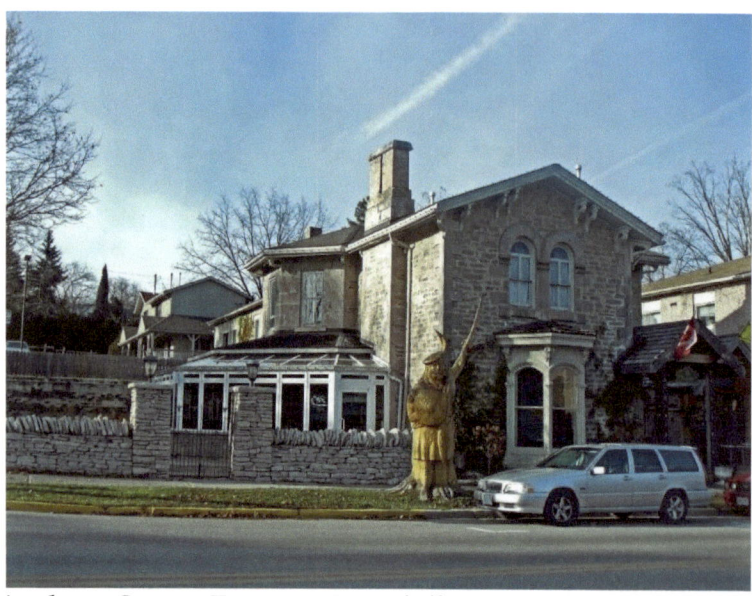

St. Andrew Street, Fergus - Breadalbane Inn - cornice brackets

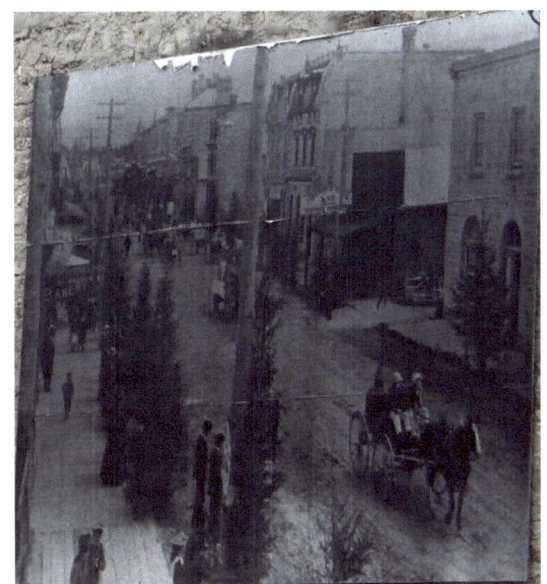

Mural – St. Andrews Street Parade c. 1890

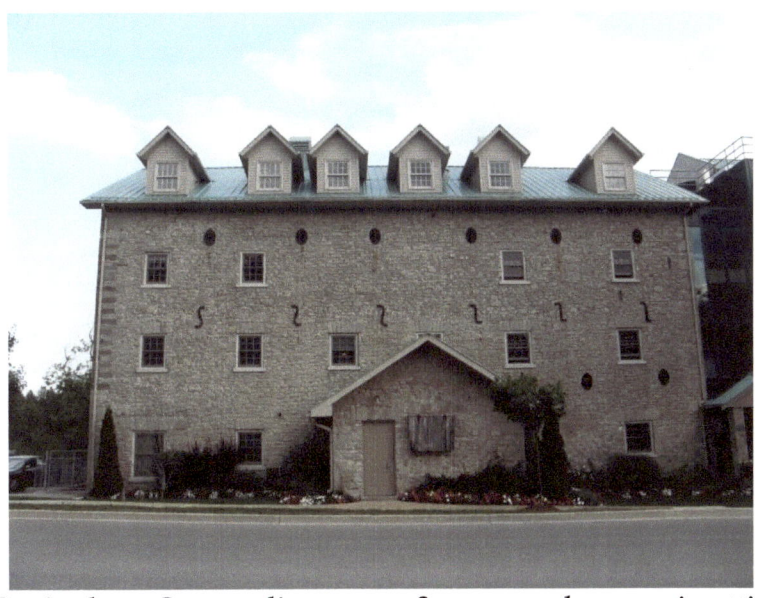

St. Andrew Street – limestone, 3 storeys, dormers in attic

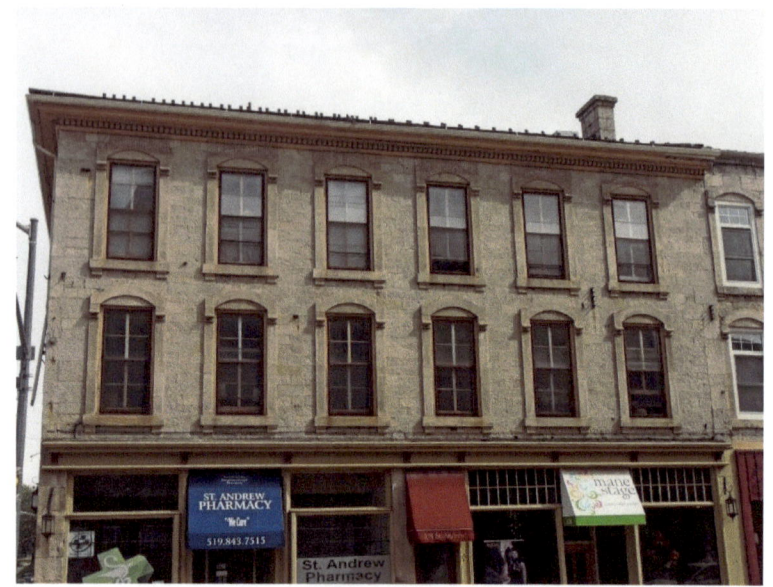

108 St. Andrew Street – Pharmacy – dentil moulding below cornice

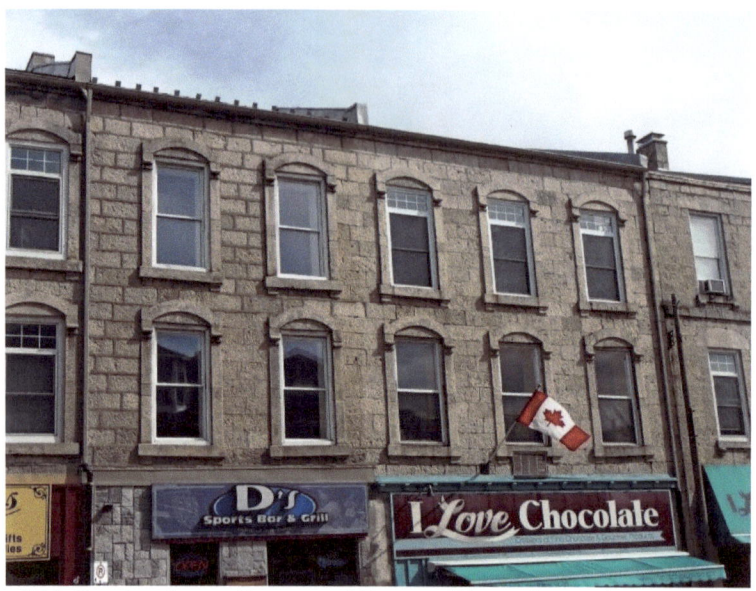

128 St. Andrew Street – I Love Chocolate - limestone

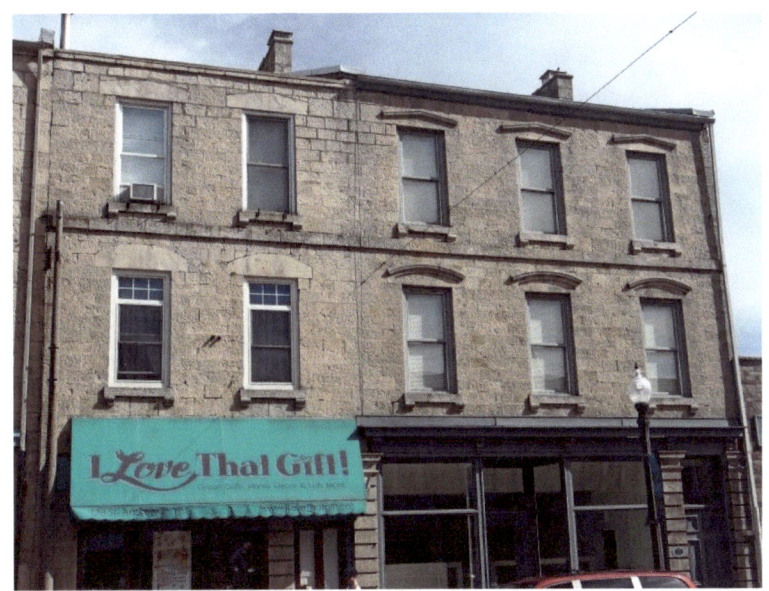

128 St. Andrew Street – I Love That Gift

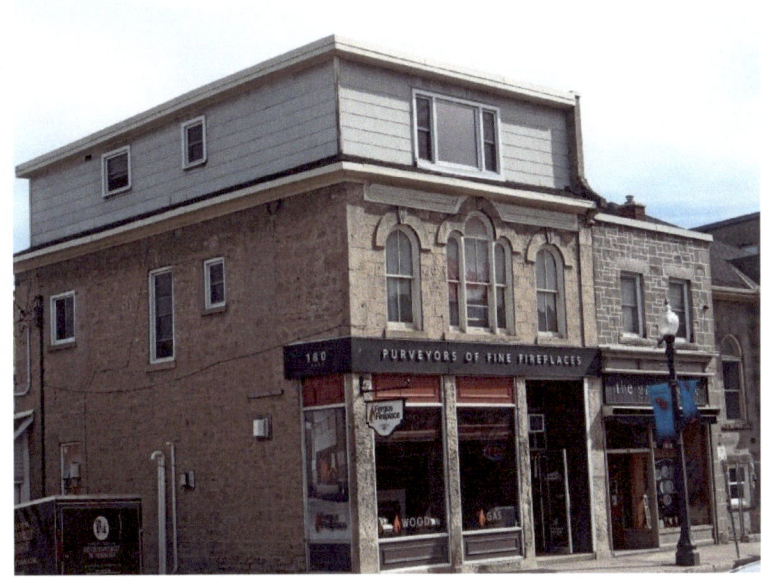

180 St. Andrew Street West – Purveyors of Fine Furniture
- limestone, semi-circular voussoirs with keystones

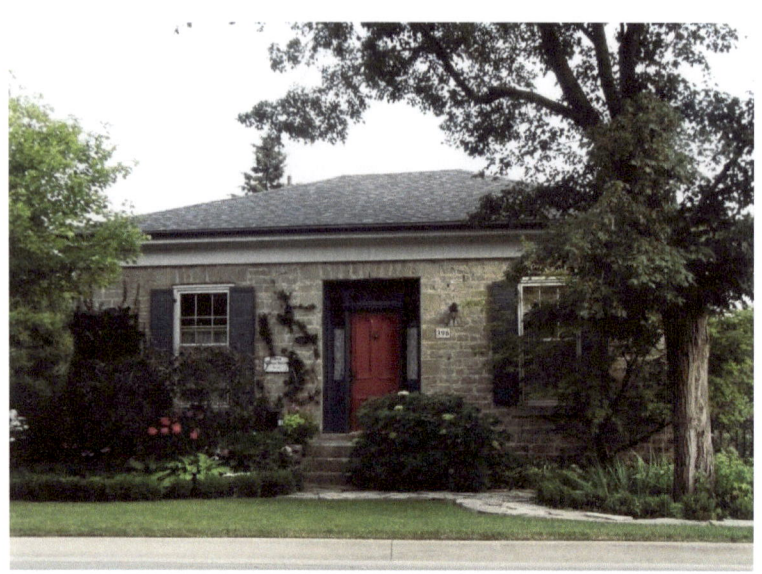

396 St. Andrew Street – William Renne, Farmer – c. 1868
Regency Cottage, hipped roof, limestone

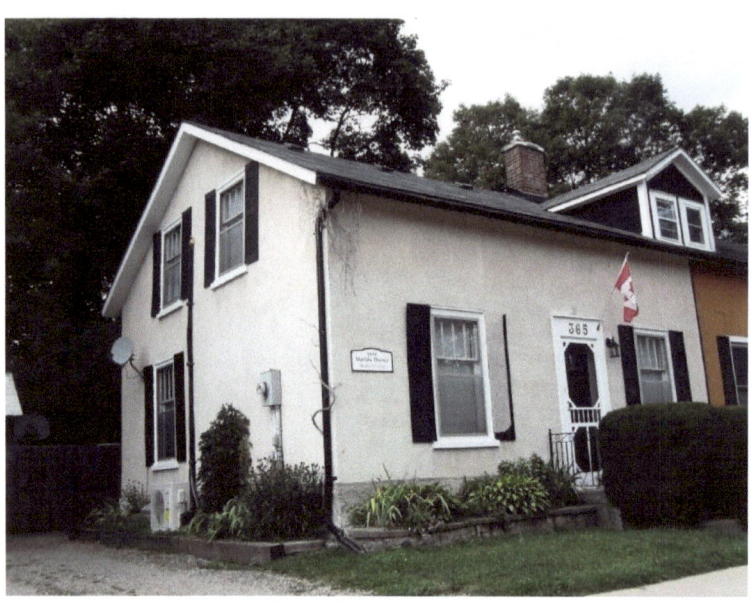

365 St. Andrew Street – Matilda Harvey, Workman's Cottage –
c. 1866 - Gothic Revival with end gable, dormer in attic, stucco

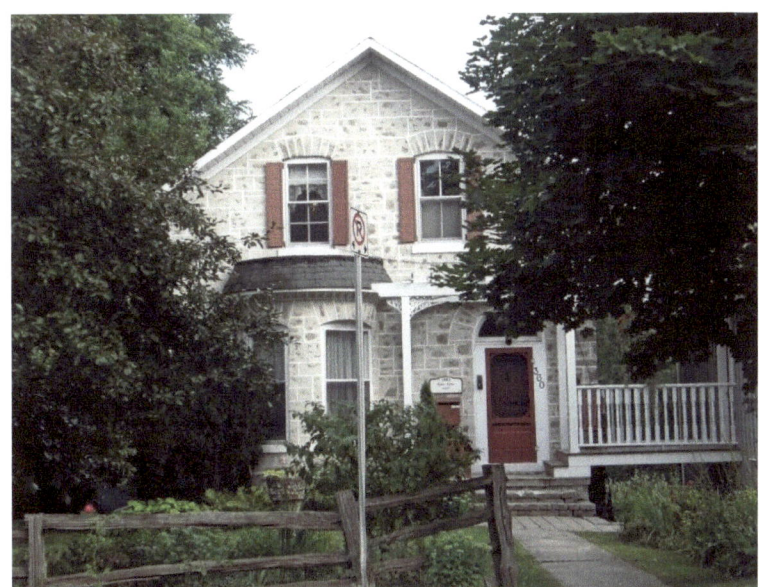

360 St. Andrew Street – John Gow, Builder – c. 1883 – bay window, voussoirs, transom window above door

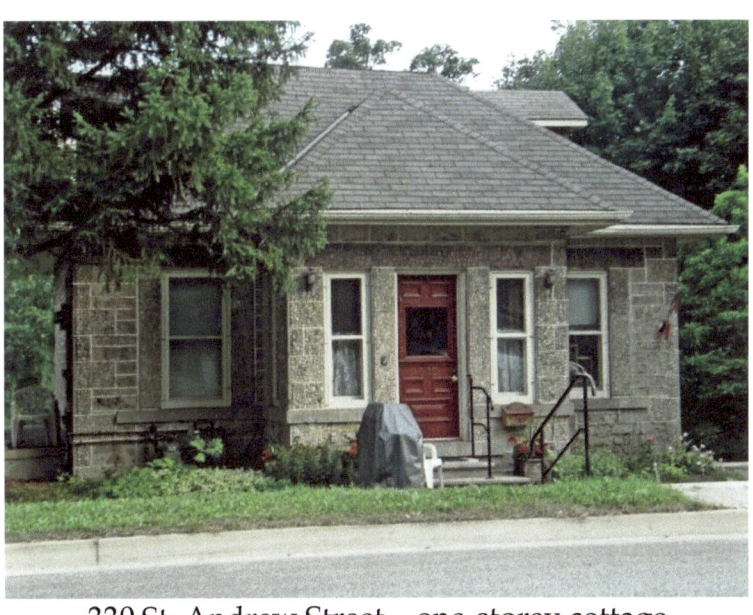

330 St. Andrew Street – one-storey cottage

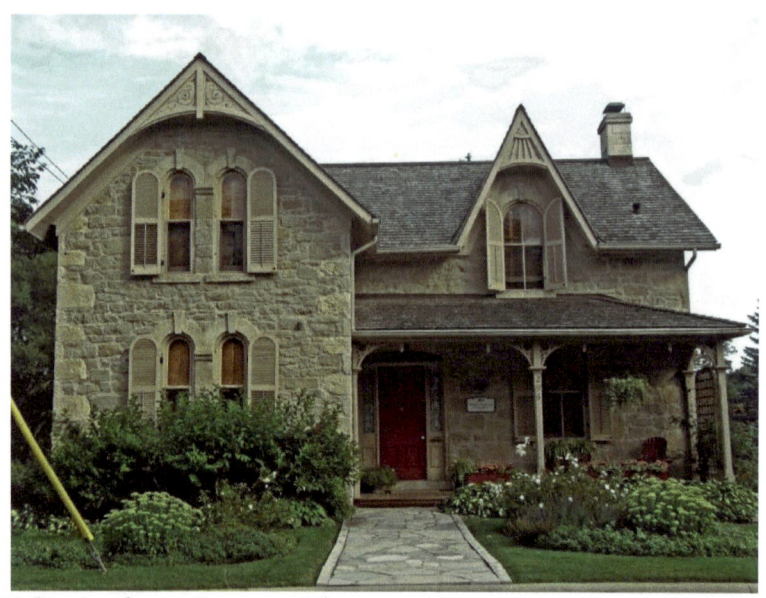

296 St. Andrew Street – Thomas Cumming, Carriage Maker – c. 1891 - Gothic Revival, verge board trim on gables, semi-circular window voussoirs with keystones, corner quoining

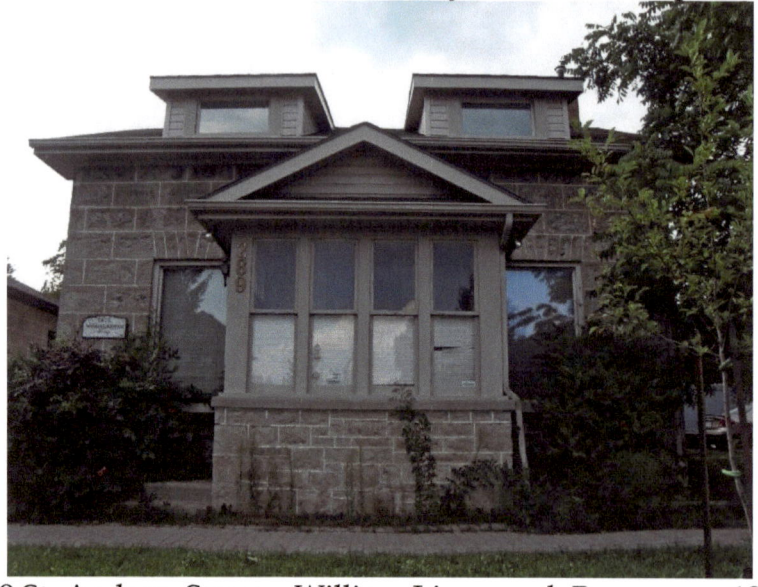

289 St. Andrew Street – William Lingwood, Brewer – c. 1873 Italianate with attic dormers, pediment above enclosed porch

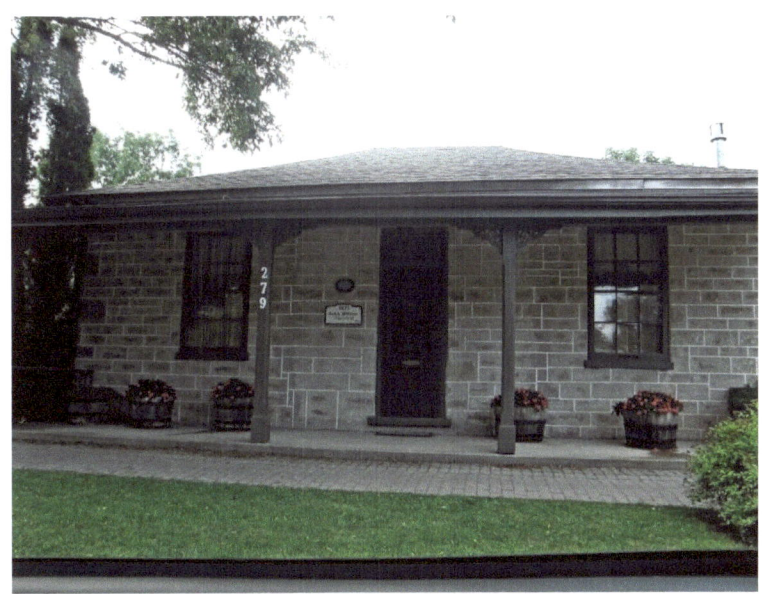

279 St. Andrew Street – John Wilson, Blacksmith – c. 1871
Regency Cottage, hipped roof

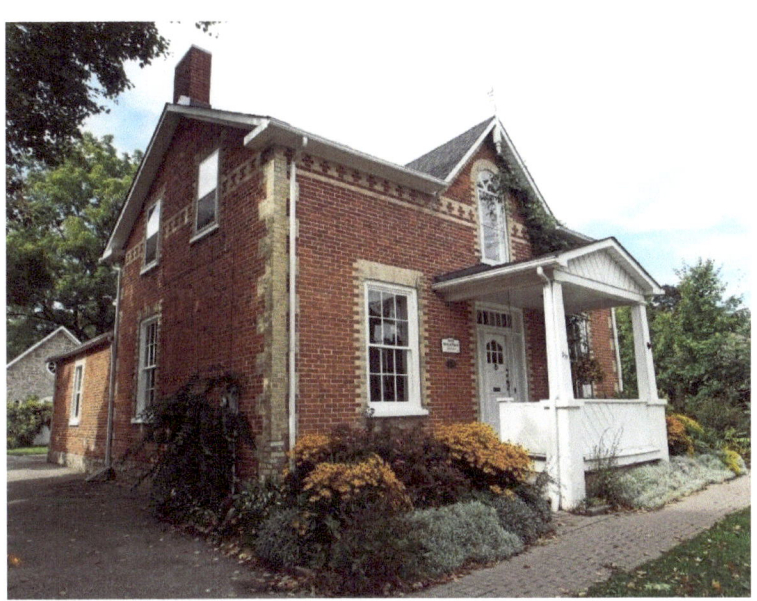

259 St. Andrew Street - c. 1868 – Gothic Revival, dichromatic
brickwork, finial on gable, cornice return on end gable
pediment above porch, corner quoins

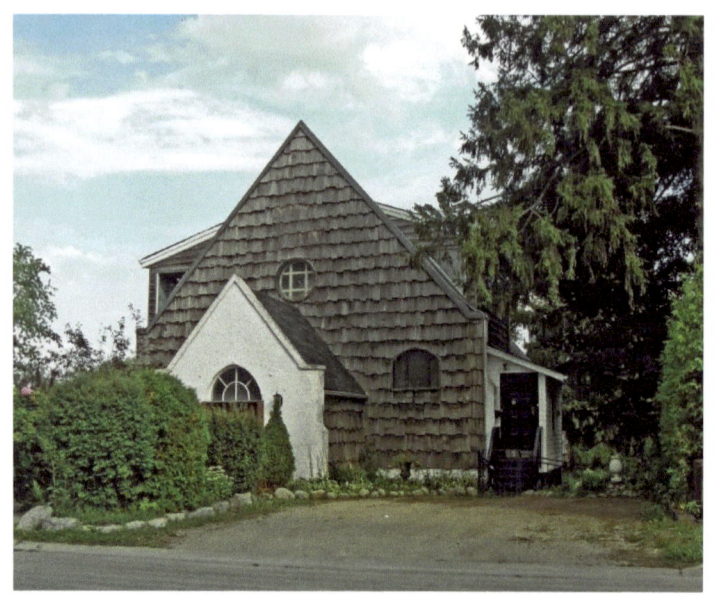

Cedar-shingle wall of cottage

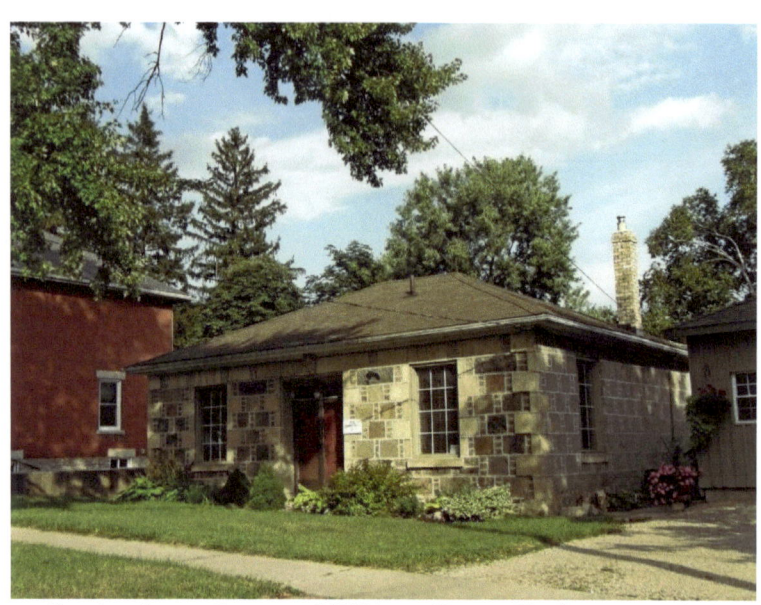

St. Andrew Street - William Dass, Tailor – c. 1875
Regency Cottage, multi-coloured brick, hipped roof

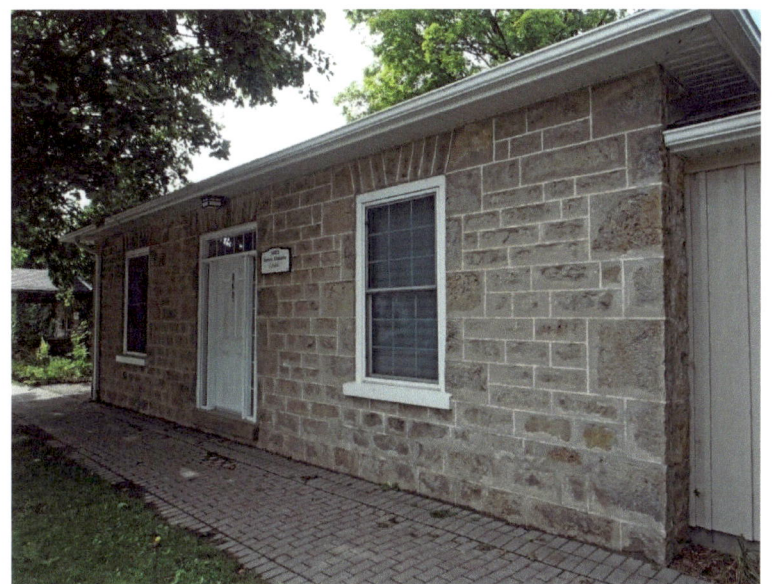

249 St. Andrew Street – James Osborne, Landlord c. 1855

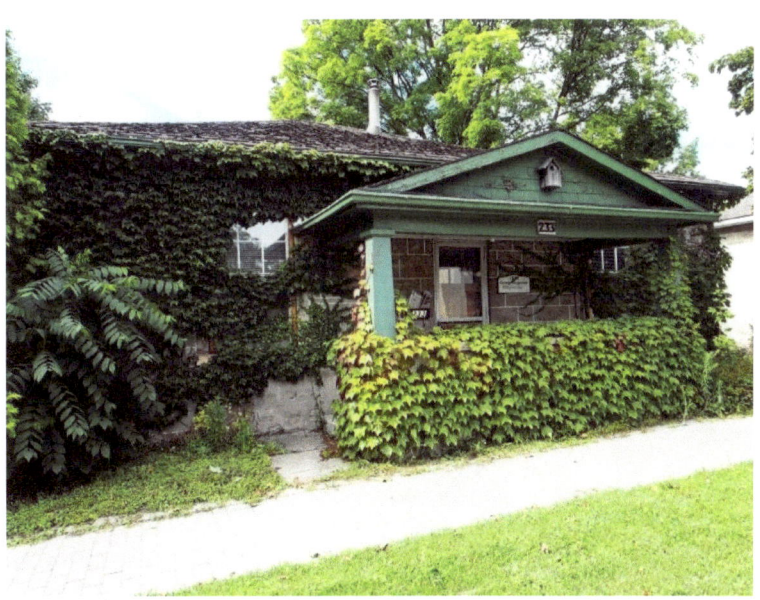

233 St. Andrew Street – George Ferguson, Workmen's Cottage
c. 1854 – hipped roof, pediment

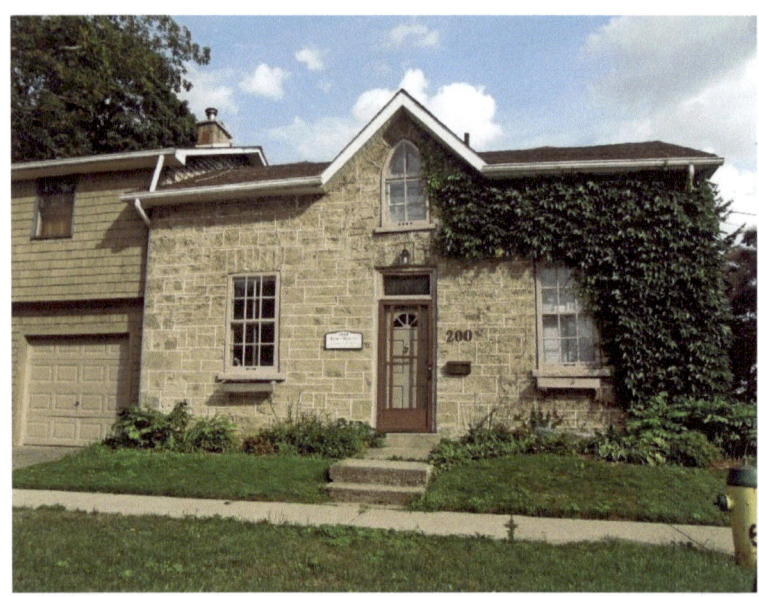

#200 – James Webster, Workman's cottage – c. 1855
- Gothic Revival – lancet window in gable, six-over-six
windows in lower storey, transom window

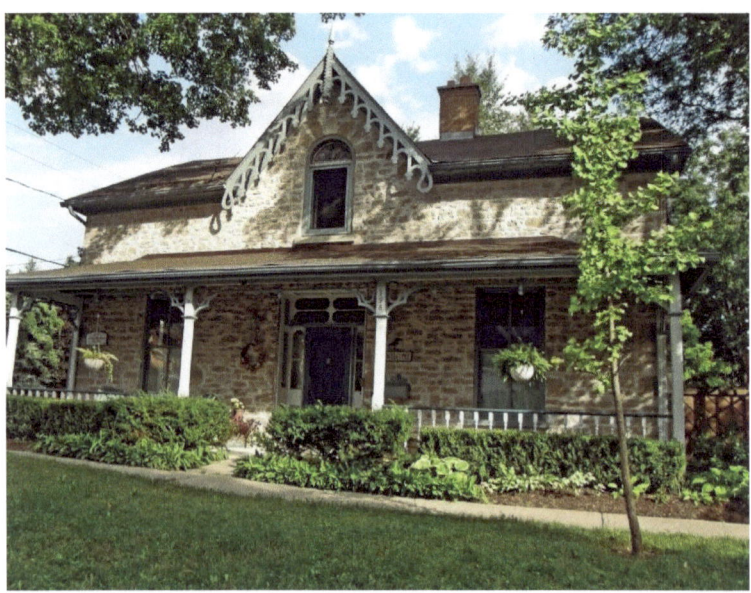

#198 St. Andrew Street – c. 1871 – Gothic Revival, verge board
trim and finial on gable, cobblestone, sidelights and transom

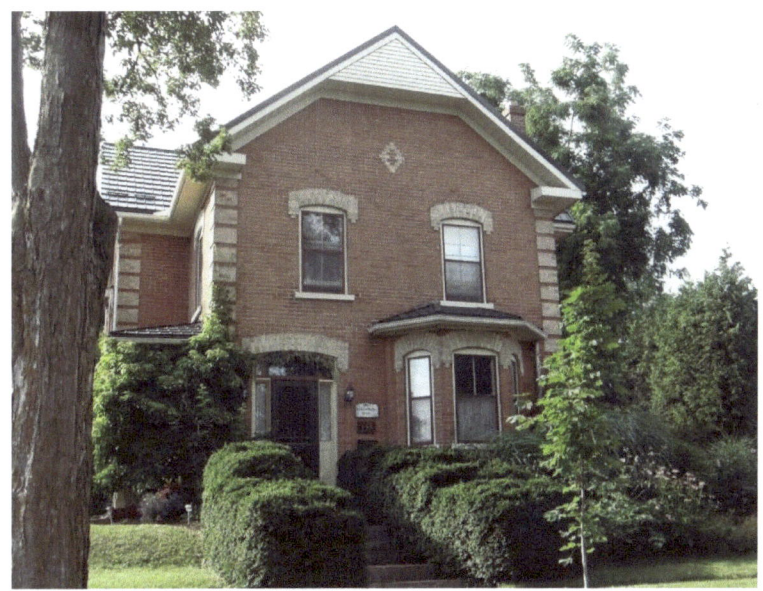

141 St. Andrew Street - James Phelan – c. 1867
Gothic Revival, corner quoins, cornice return on gable, bay
window, dichromatic brickwork

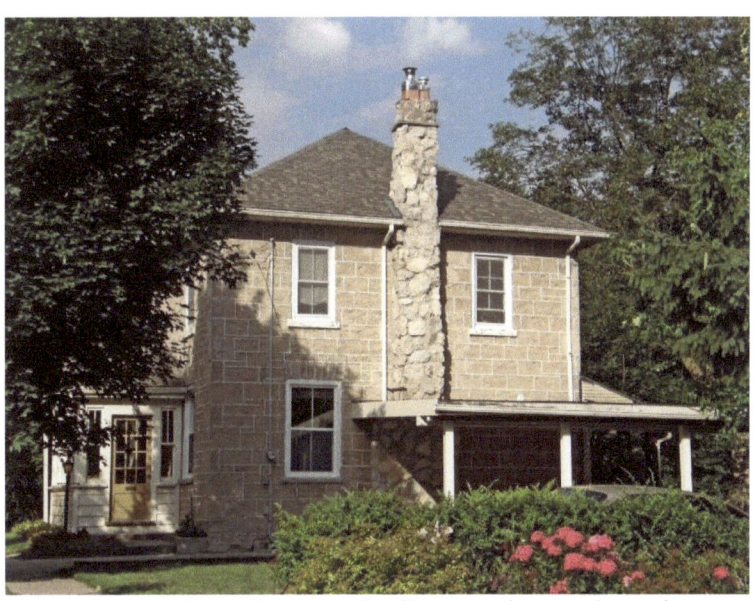

St. Andrew Street – Italianate, hipped roof

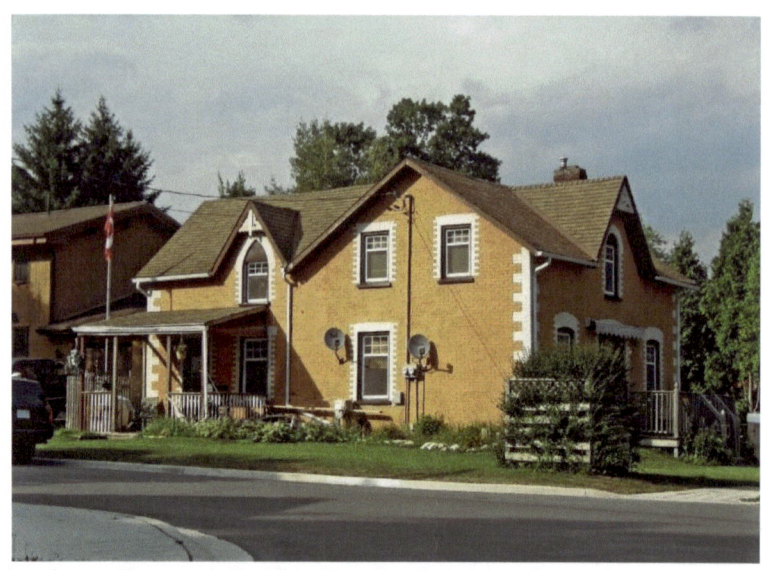

St. Andrew Street - Gothic Revival, verge board trim on gables with lancet windows, corner quoins

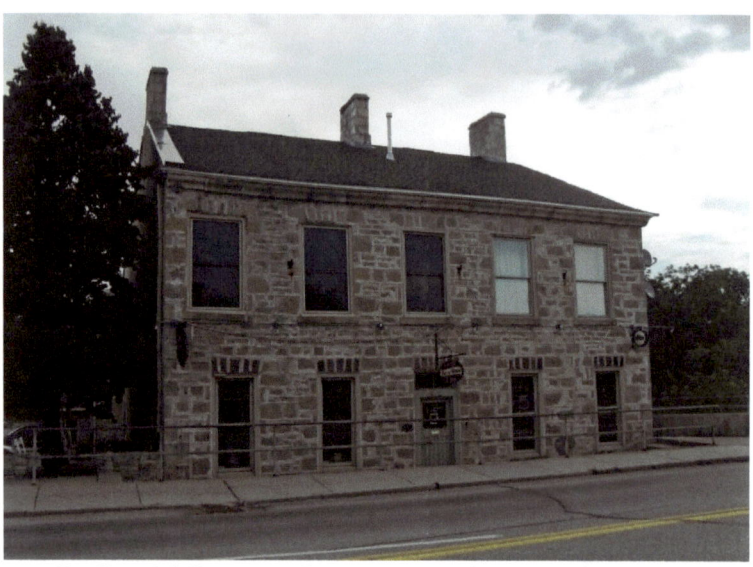

St. David Street - Georgian style stone building

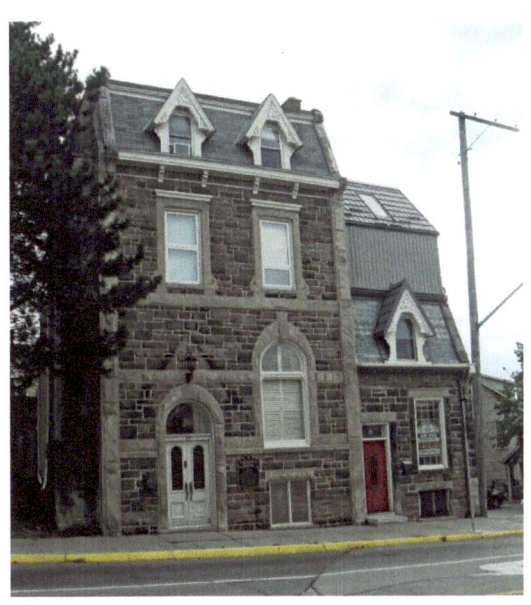

St. David Street

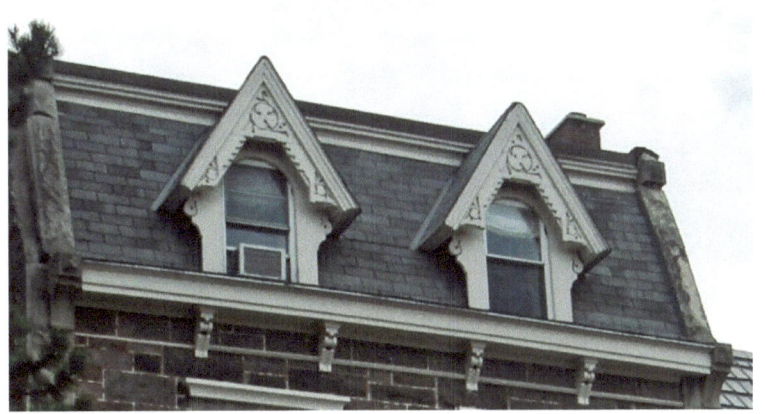

Decorative gabled window hoods on dormers,
single cornice brackets

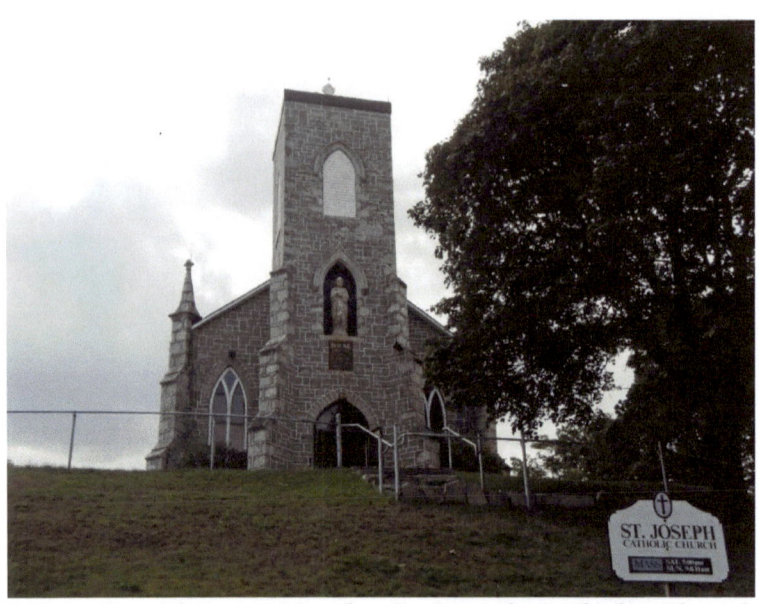

760 St. David Street North - St. Joseph Catholic Church
– lancet windows, buttresses

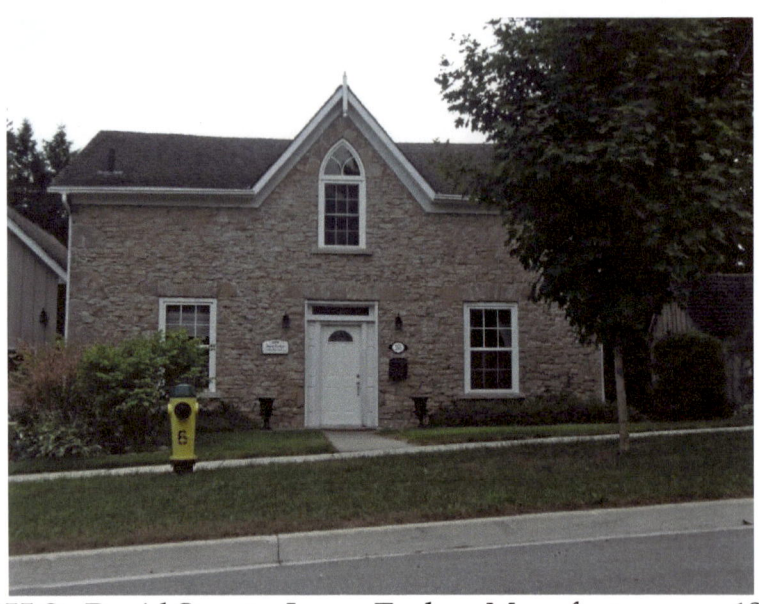

#255 St. David Street – James Tocher, Manufacturer - c. 1882
Gothic cottage, finial on gable, lancet window in gable

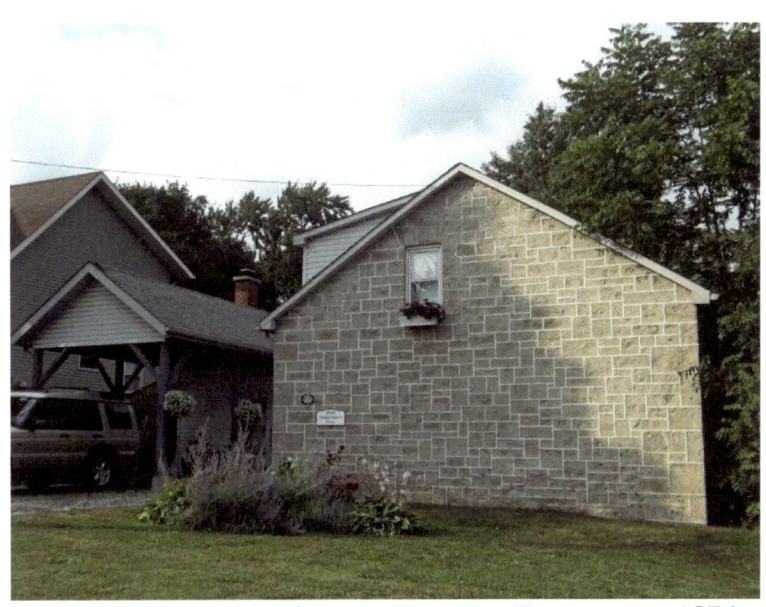

St. David Street - Thomas Dow Jr., Farmer – c. 1856

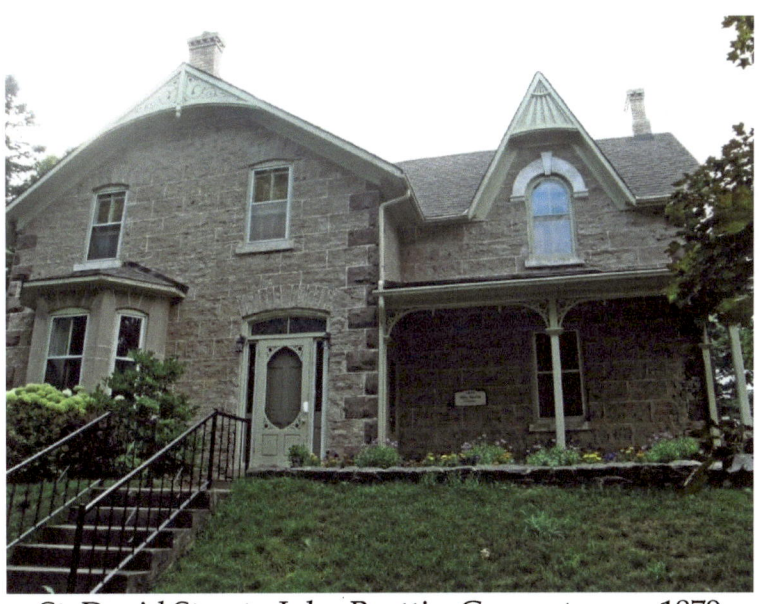

St. David Street - John Beattie, Carpenter – c. 1879
Verge board trim on gables with final, corner quoin, sidelights
and transom windows, bay window, arched window voussoir
with keystone

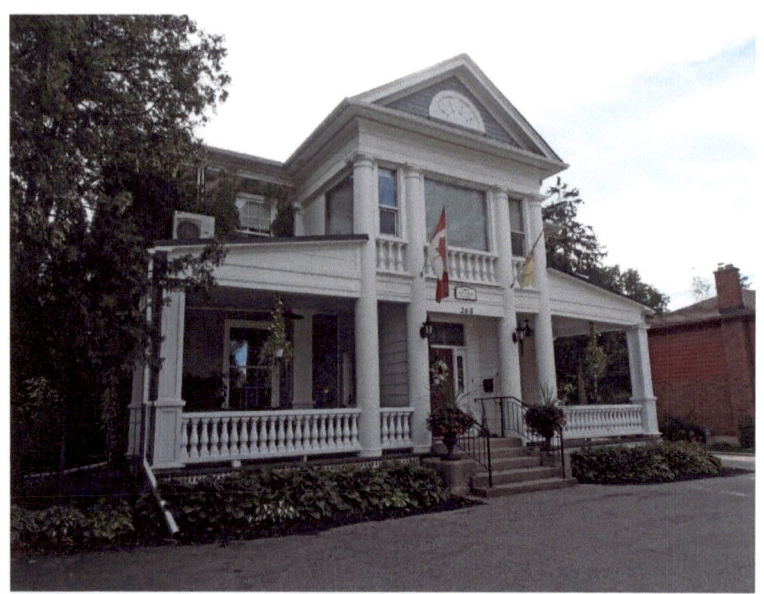

265 St. David Street North - James Argo Merchant c. 1867
Neocolonial style - hipped roof, two-storey-tall Doric porch
pillars topped with pediment with decorated tympanum

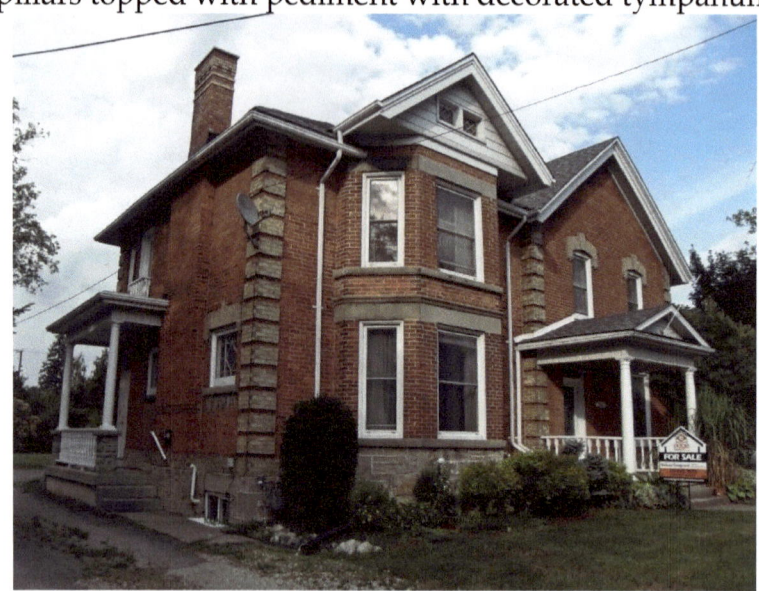

#250 St. David Street – Edwardian/Gothic – corner quoins,
arched window voussoirs with keystones, pediment

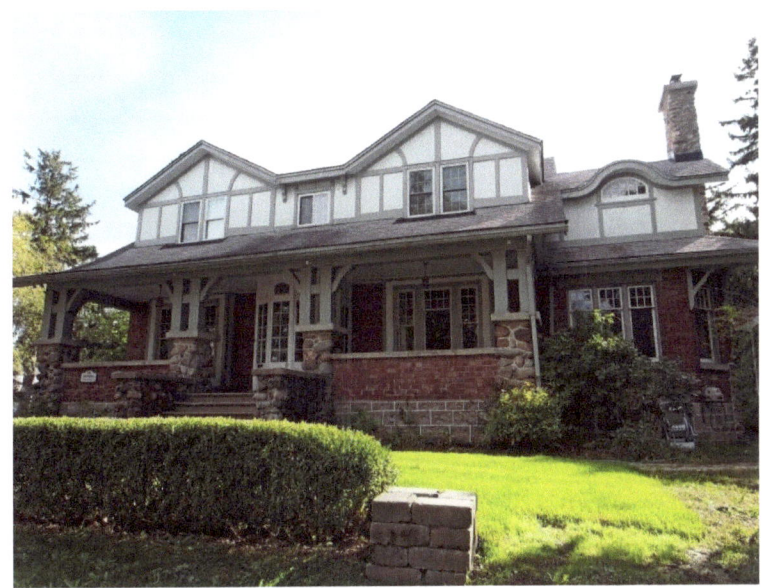

St. David Street - W. G. Beatty, Foundry – c. 1912 – Tudor style

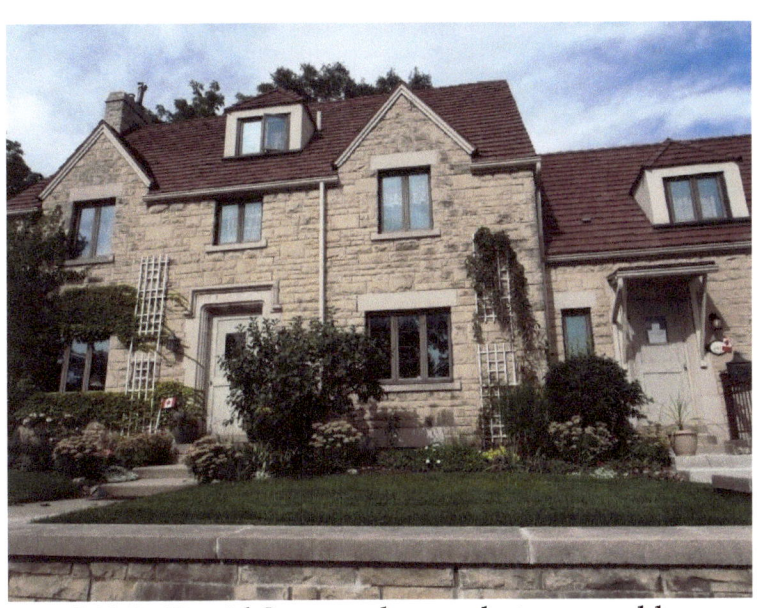

240 St. David Street – dormer between gables

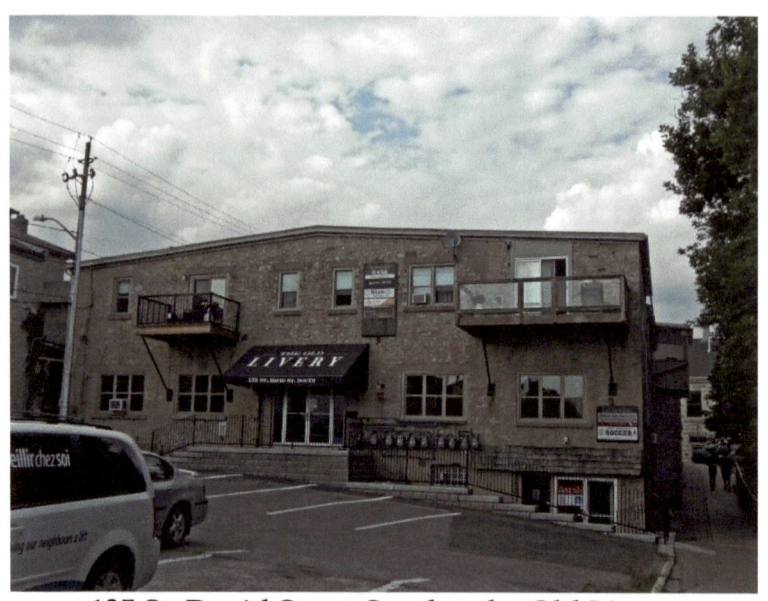

135 St. David Street South – the Old Livery

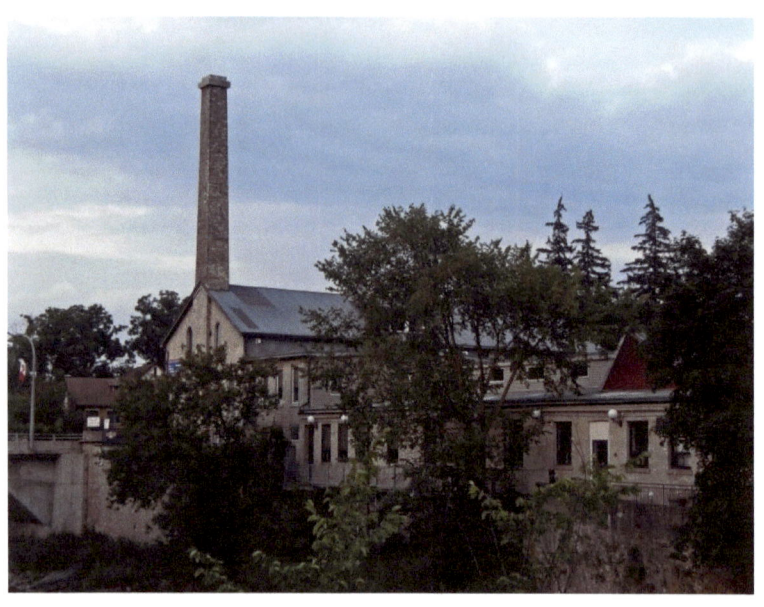

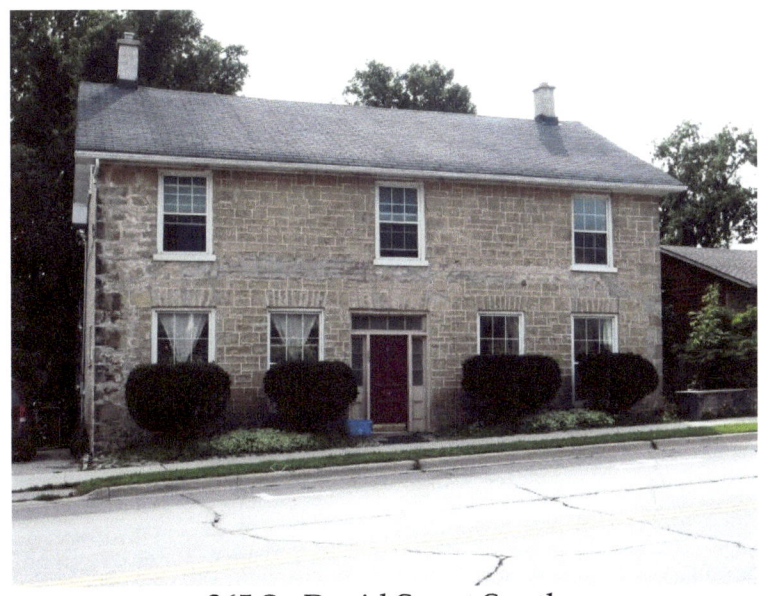

265 St. David Street South

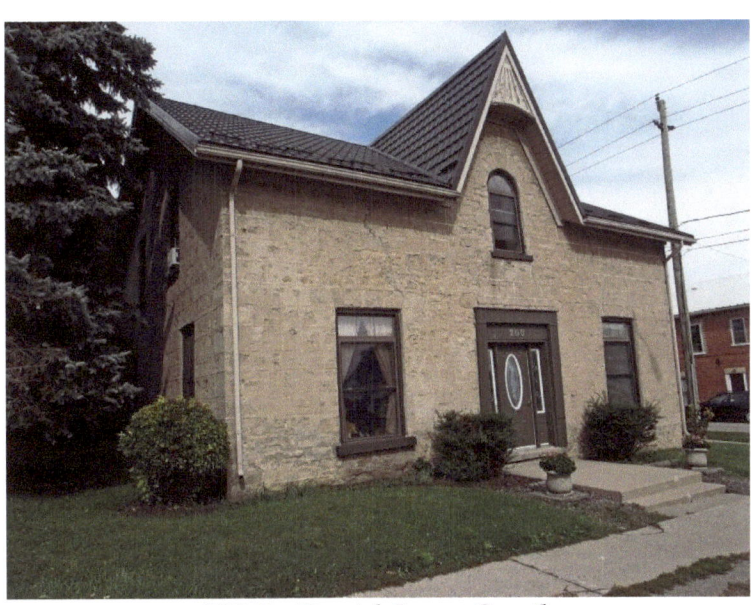

200 St. David Street South

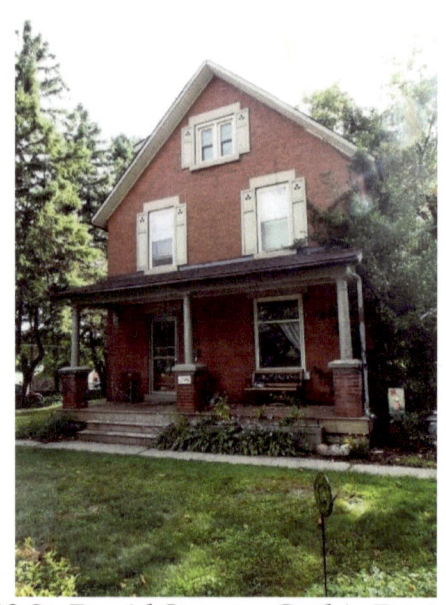

399 St. David Street – Gothic Revival

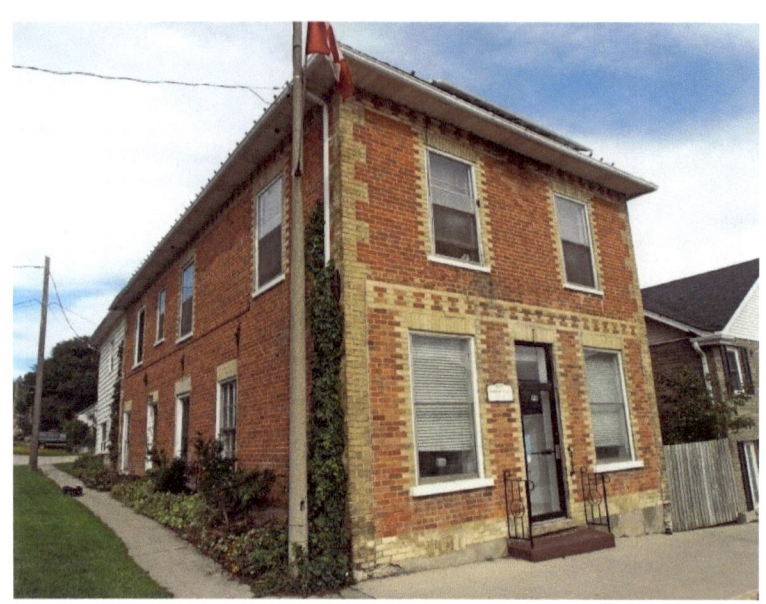

198 St. David Street – Johanna Bergin, Seamstress c. 1871 – hipped roof, dichromatic brick work, and corner quoins

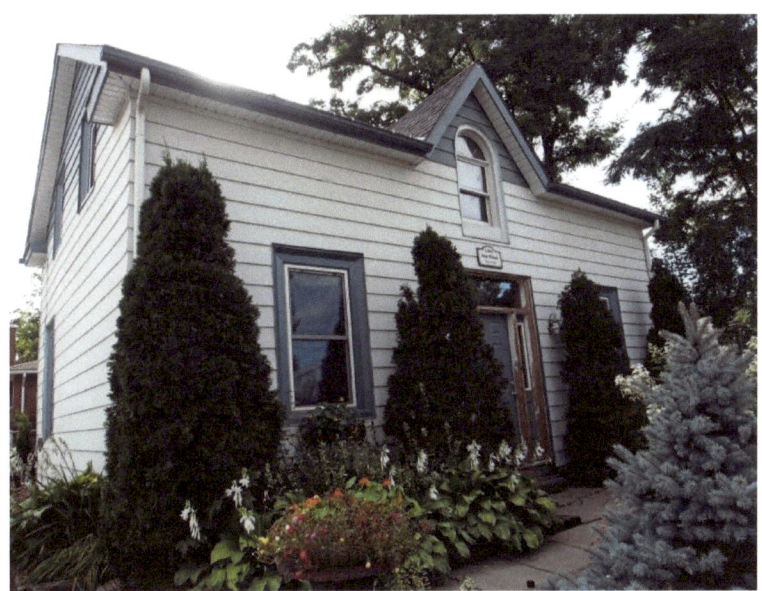

205 St. David Street – John Wilson, Blacksmith c. 1860
Gothic Revival

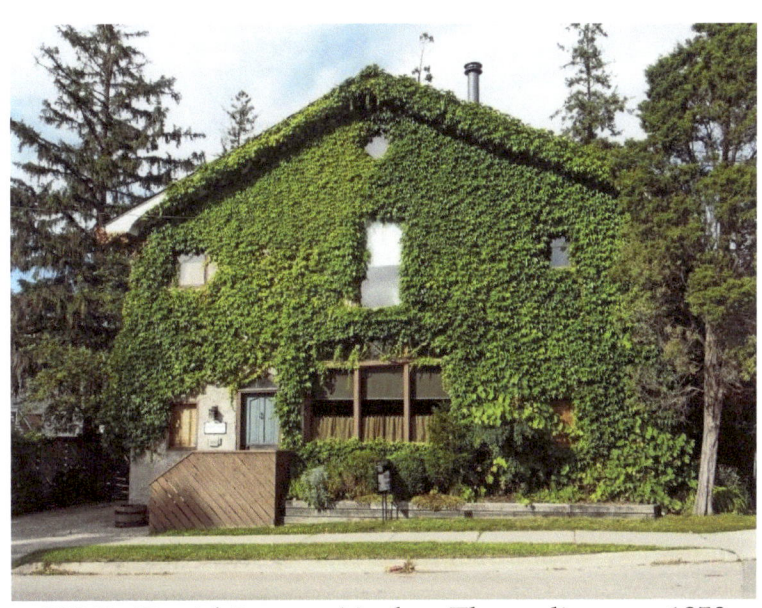

290 St. David Street – Yankee Thorp, livery c. 1859

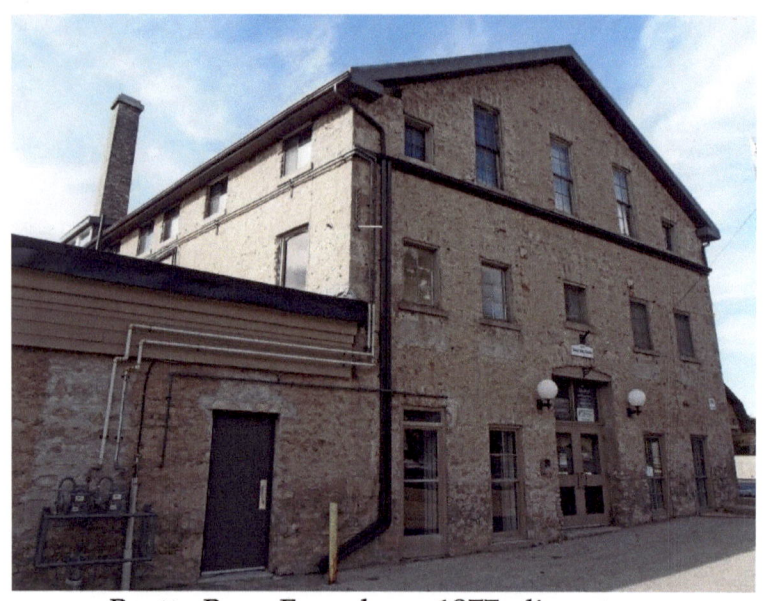

Beatty Bros. Foundry c. 1877 - limestone

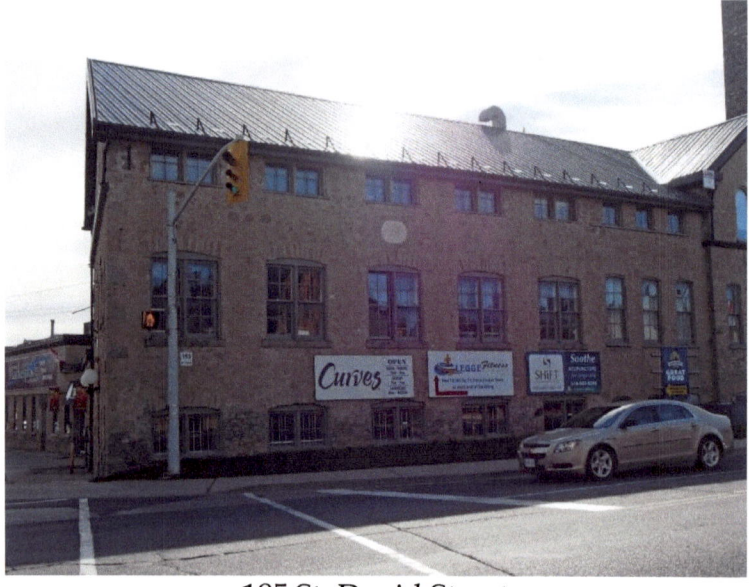

195 St. David Street

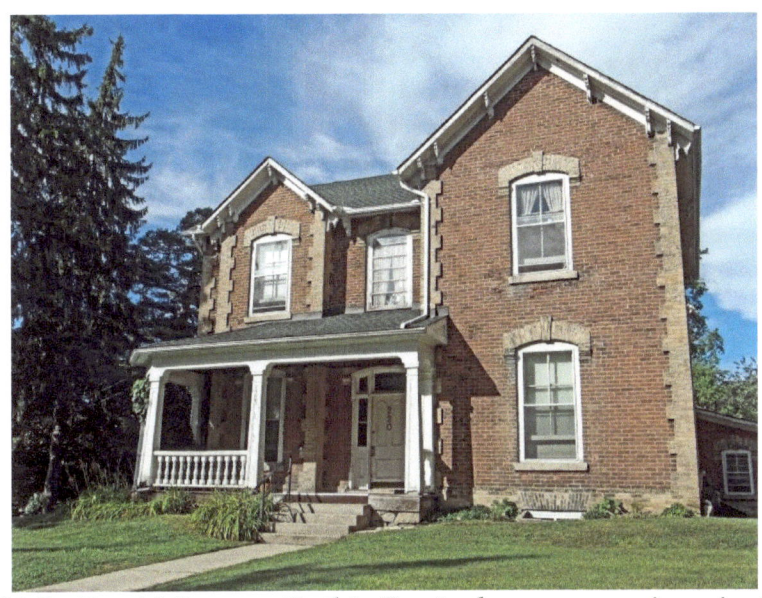

220 St. David Street – Gothic Revival, corner quoins, single cornice brackets

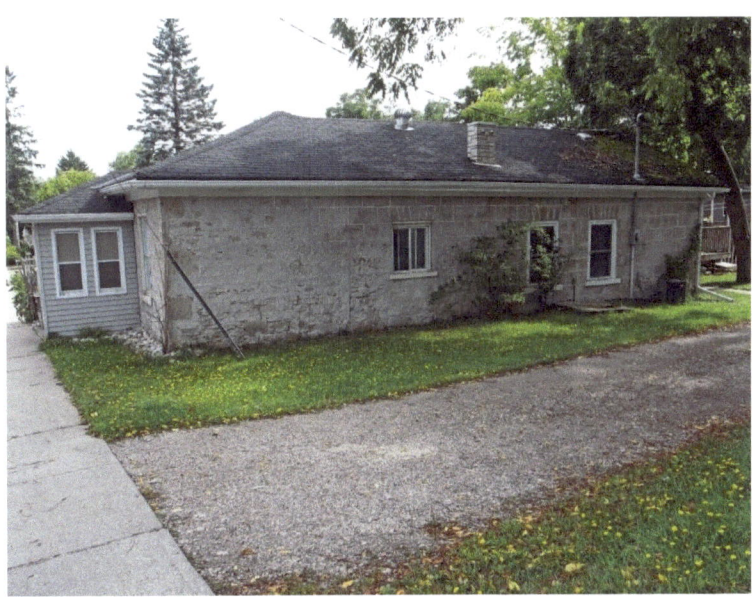

191 Cameron Street – William Cardy, Farmer c. 1877 – Regency Cottage, hipped roof, limestone

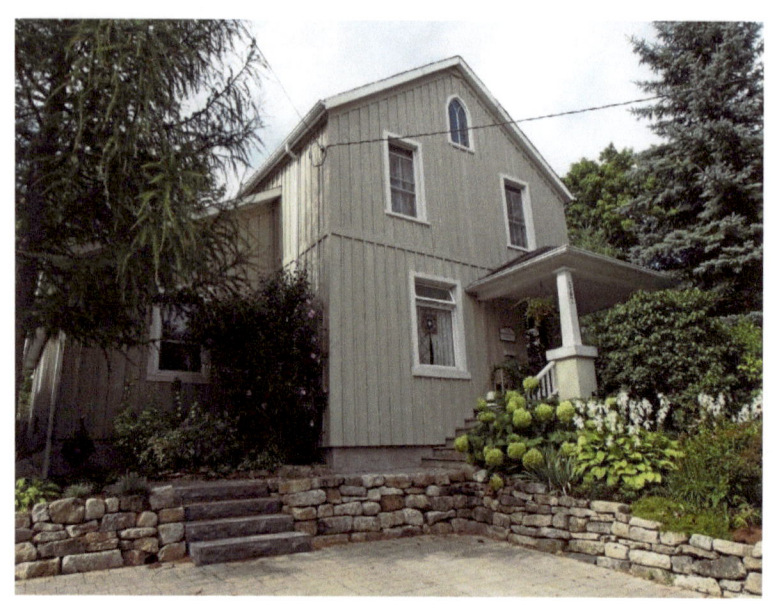

367 St. Patrick Street

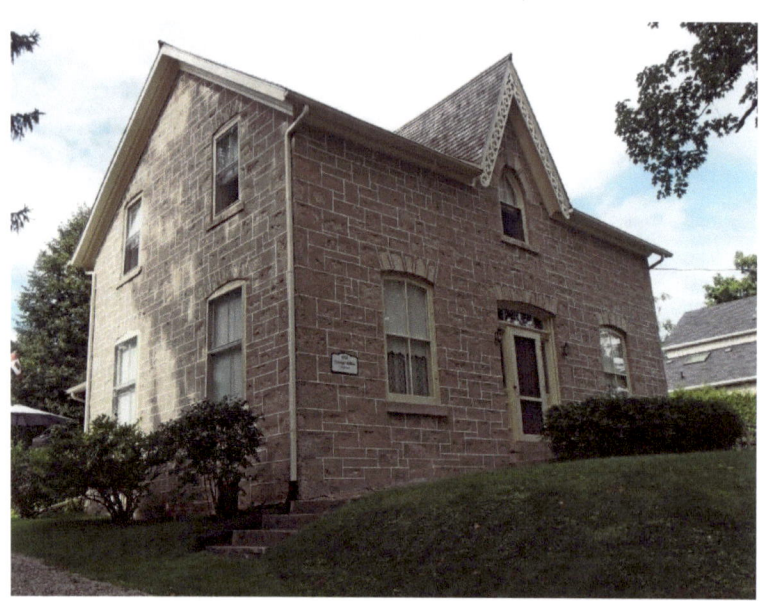

351 St. Patrick Street - George Wilkie, Carpenter – c. 1872
Gothic Revival

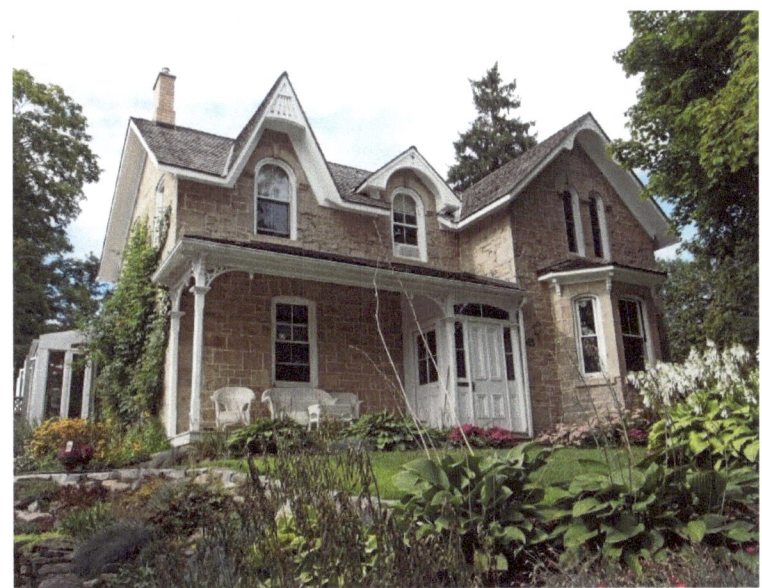

345 St. Patrick Street – Gothic Revival, semi-circular windows with voussoirs and keystones on upper storey, bay window

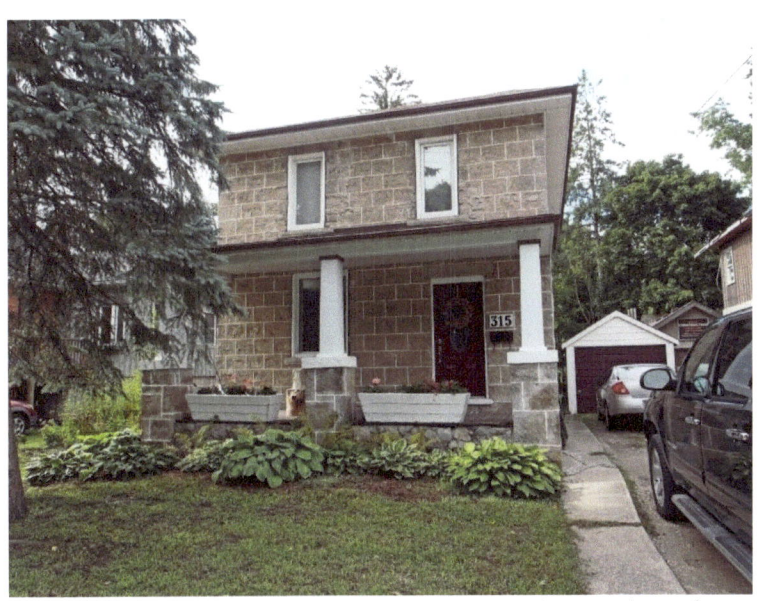

315 St. Patrick Street – two-storey, hipped roof

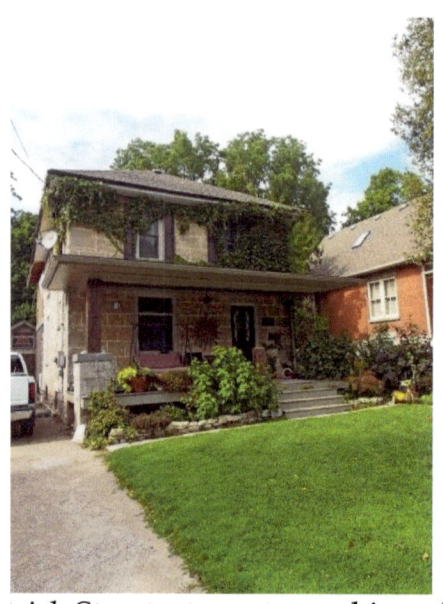

St. Patrick Street – two-storey, hipped roof

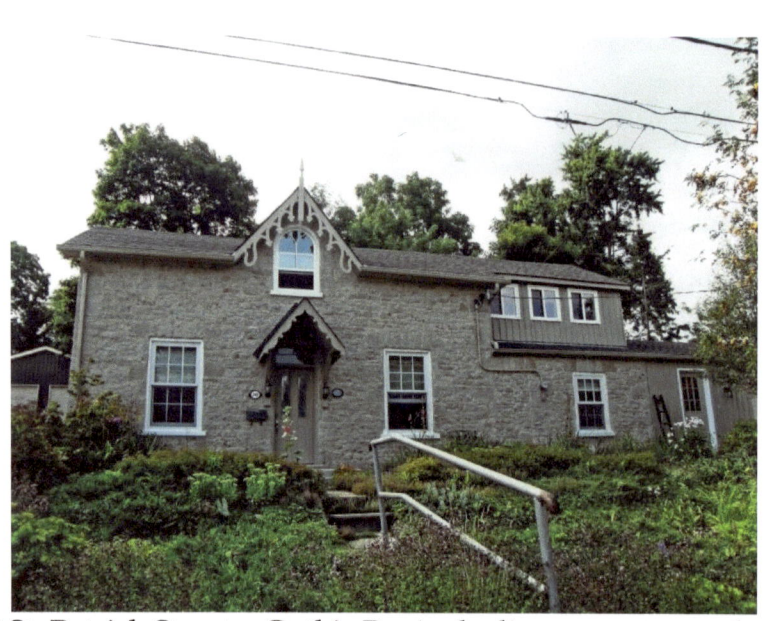

249 St. Patrick Street – Gothic Revival – limestone, verge board
trim on gable with finial

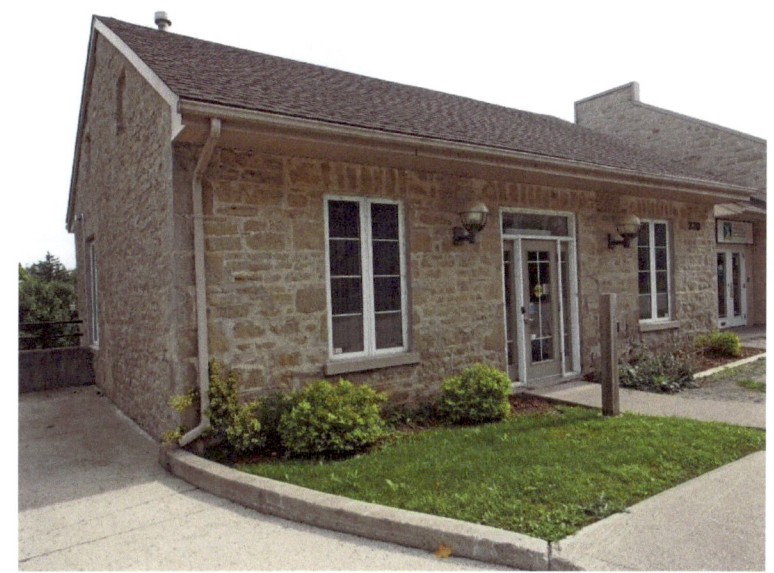

238 St. Patrick Street – Regency Cottage – sidelights, transom

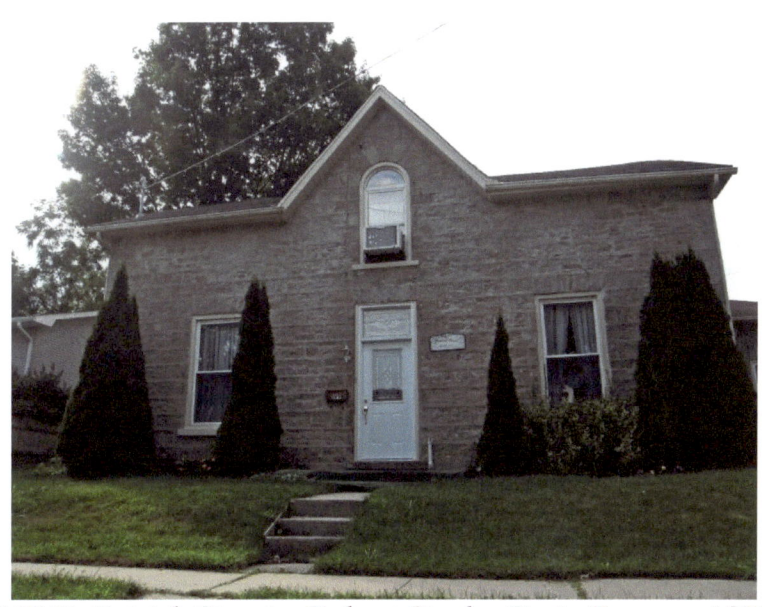

199 St. Patrick Street – Robert Steele, Grain Buyer c. 1871
Gothic cottage

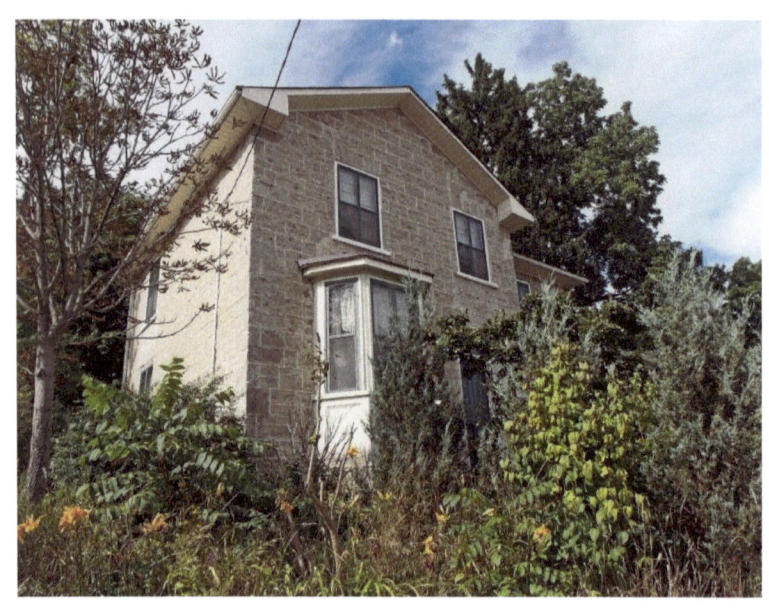

203 St. Patrick Street – Rev. Enoch Barker, Minister c. 1870

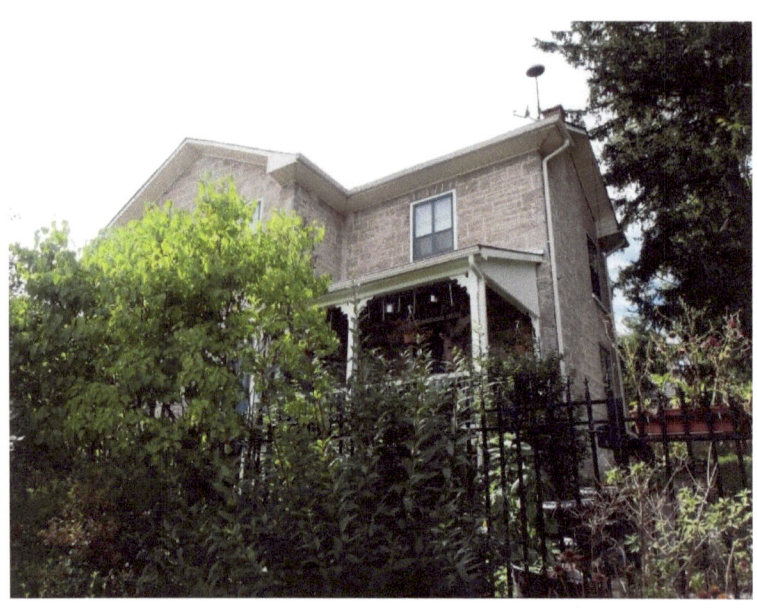

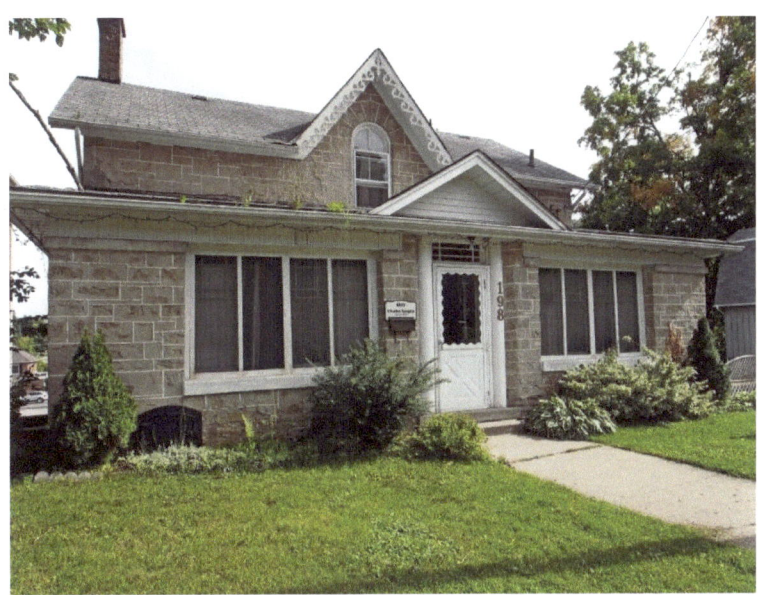

198 St. Patrick Street – Charles Templin, Carriage Maker
c. 1877 – verge board trim on gable,
transom window above door

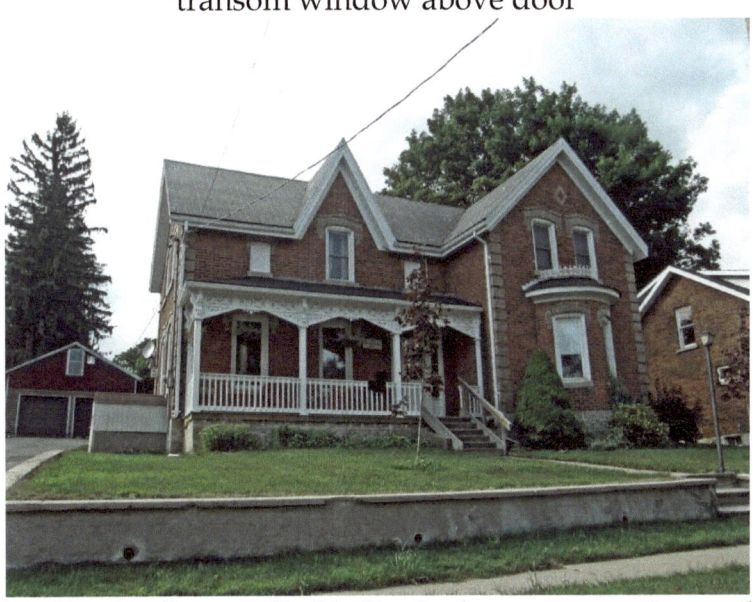

155 St. Patrick Street - Gothic Revival – corner quoins, arched
window voussoirs, iron cresting above bay window

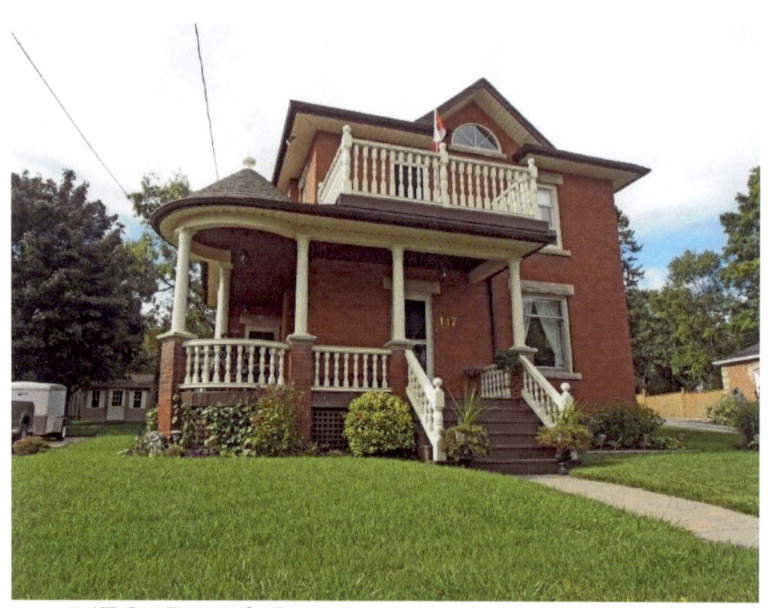

147 St. Patrick Street – wraparound verandah,
second floor balcony

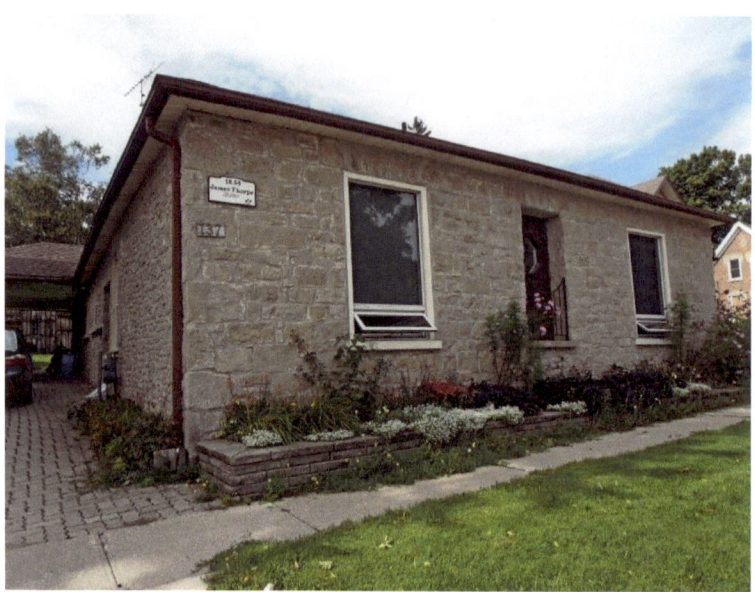

137 St. Patrick Street – James Thorpe, Hostler – c. 1854
– Regency Cottage - hipped roof

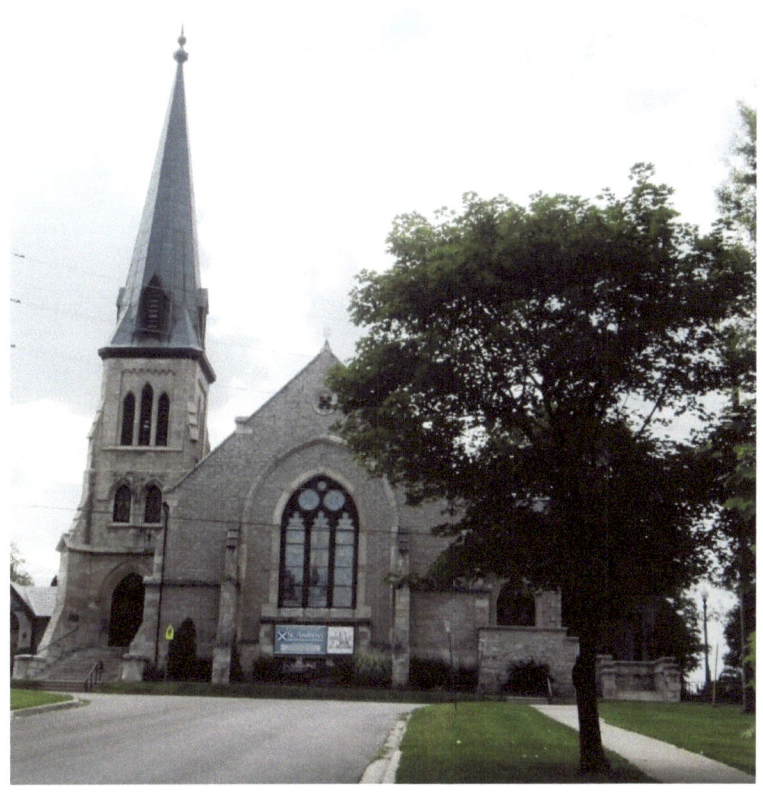

325 St. George Street West - St. Andrew's Presbyterian
Church, prominently situated on a hilltop overlooking Fergus,
was the dominant visual landmark as well as the religious
focus of this Scottish community during the second half of the
19th century. It was erected in 1862 to serve a congregation
established almost 30 years before and replaced an earlier
church that stood on the site. Built of locally quarried stone,
this attractive Gothic Revival structure is distinguished by its
high-pitched roof, massive buttresses and elegant spire.

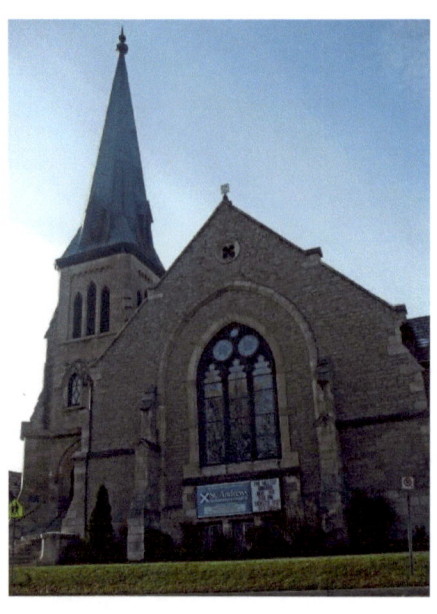

St. Andrew's Presbyterian Church, Fergus

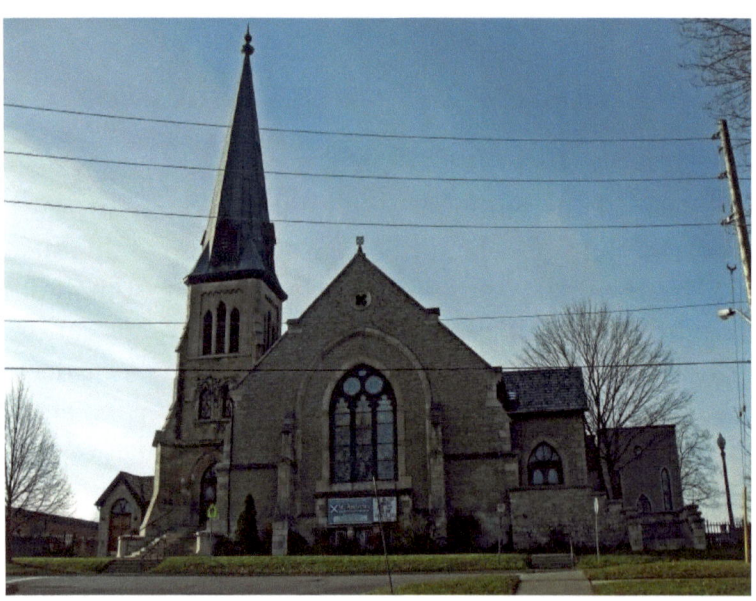

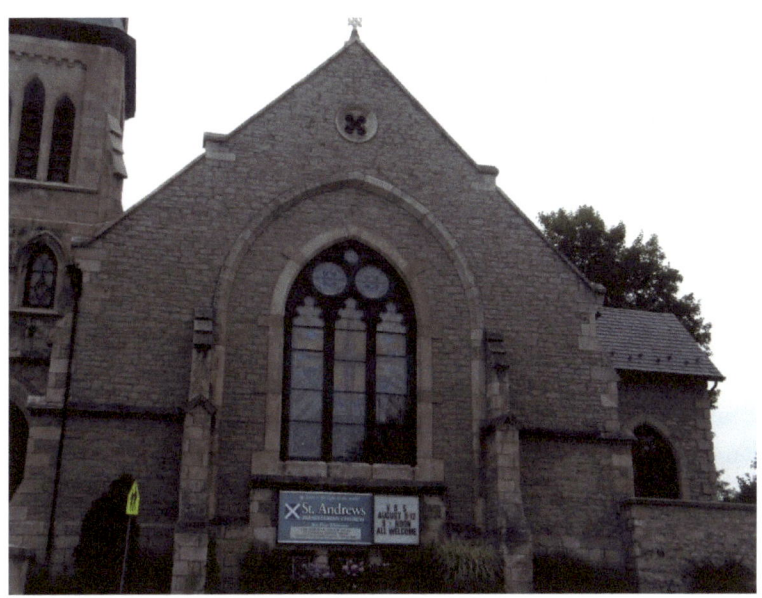

Rose windows, stained glass windows

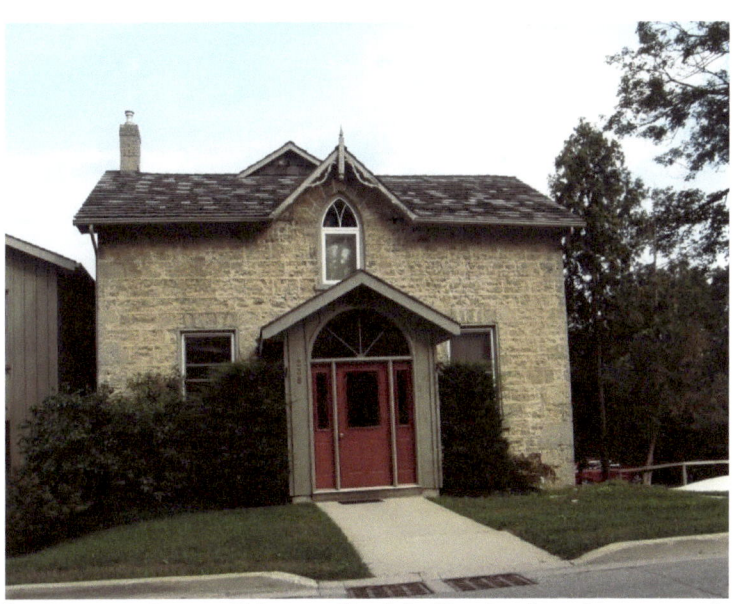

238 St. George Street West – Gothic Revival style, verge board trim and finial

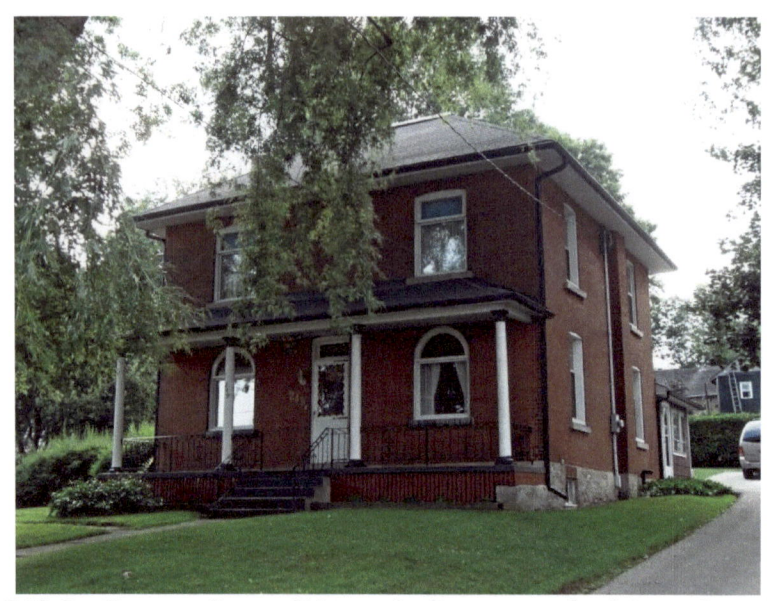
249 St. George Street West – Italianate style, hipped roof

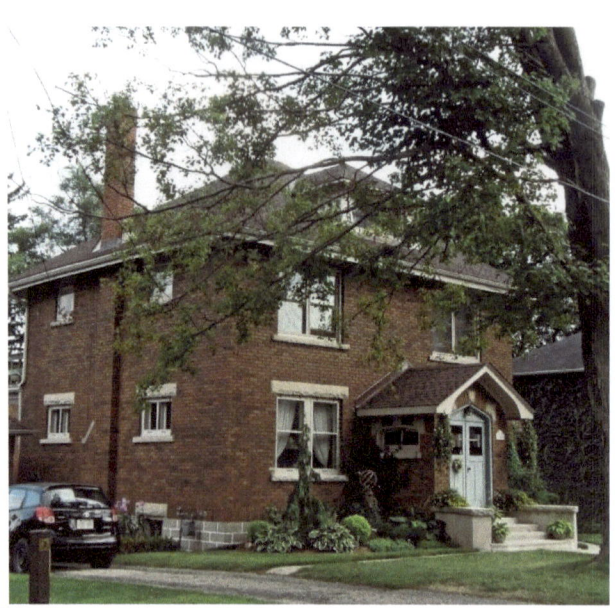
150 St. George Street West – Italianate, dormer in attic

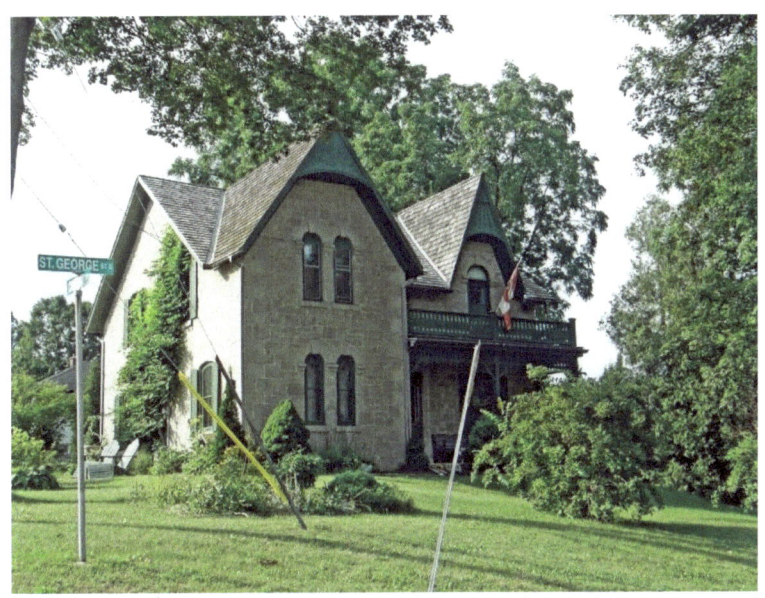

St. George Street – Gothic Revival, verge board trim on gables, balcony on second floor

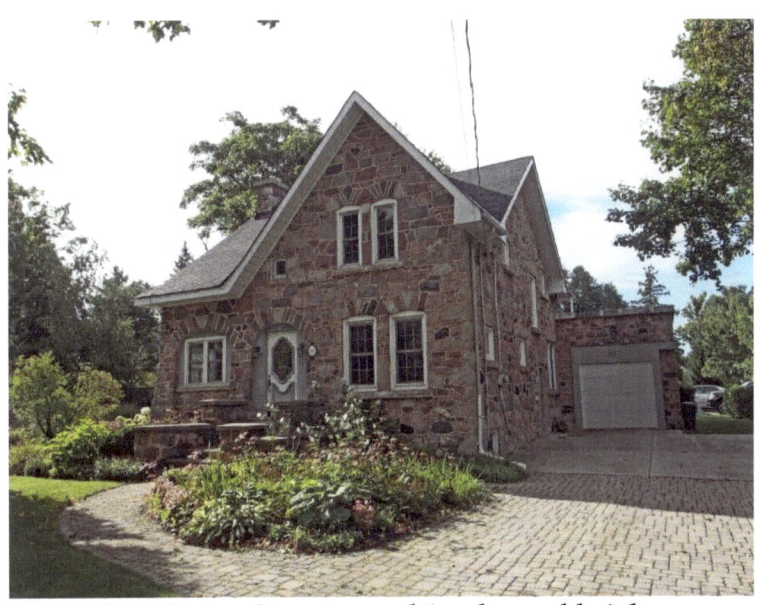

361 Union Street – multi-coloured bricks

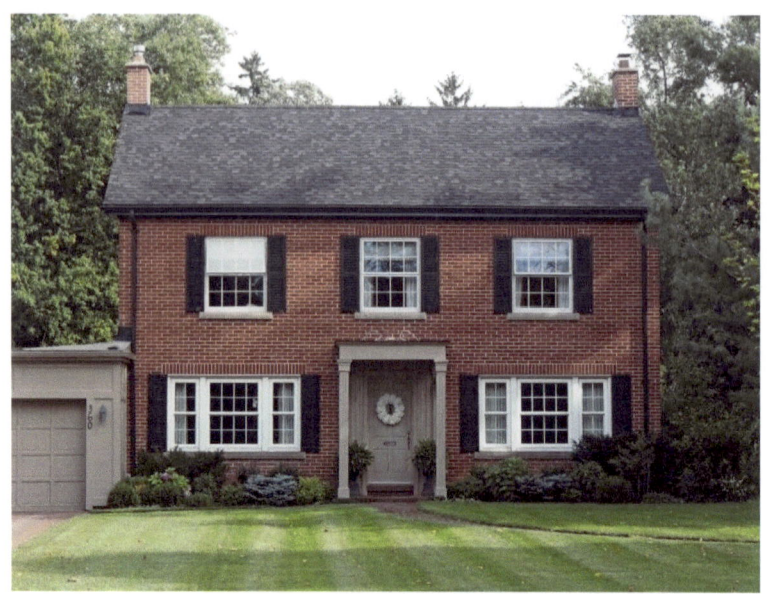

360 Union Street – Georgian style, multi-paned windows

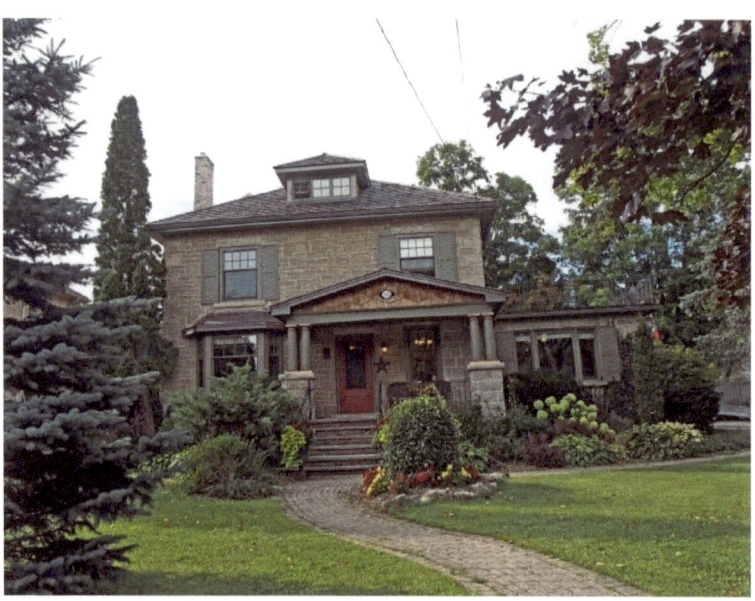

345 Union Street – two storeys, dormer, pediment

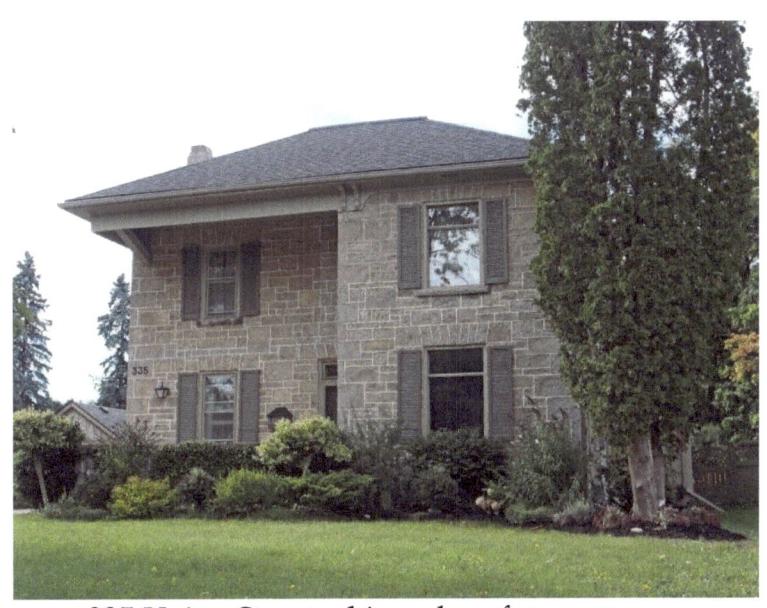

335 Union Street – hipped roof, two storeys

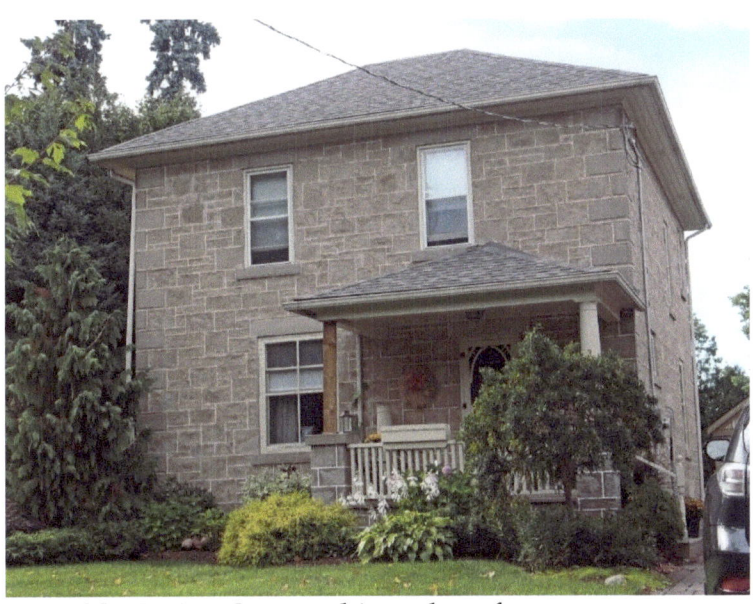

325 Union Street – hipped roof, two storeys

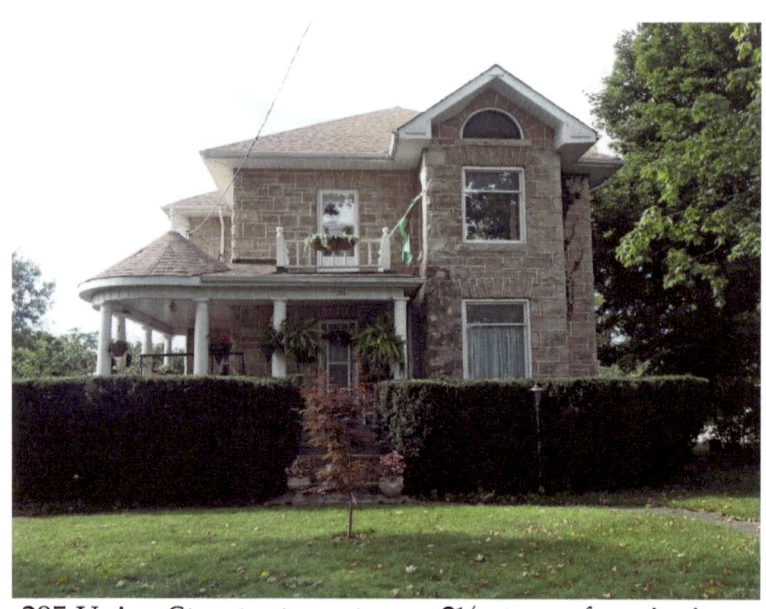

295 Union Street – two storey, 2½ storey frontispiece, wraparound verandah

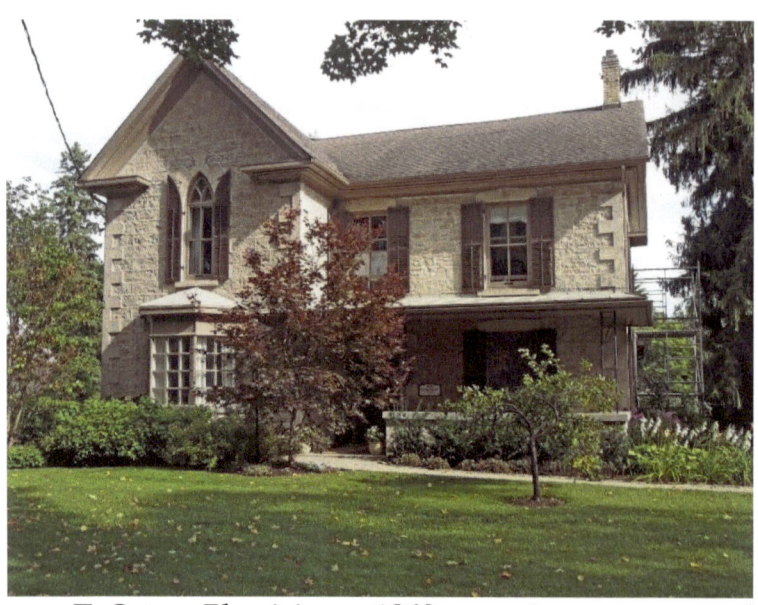

George T. Orton, Physician c. 1869 – cornice return on gable, corner quoins

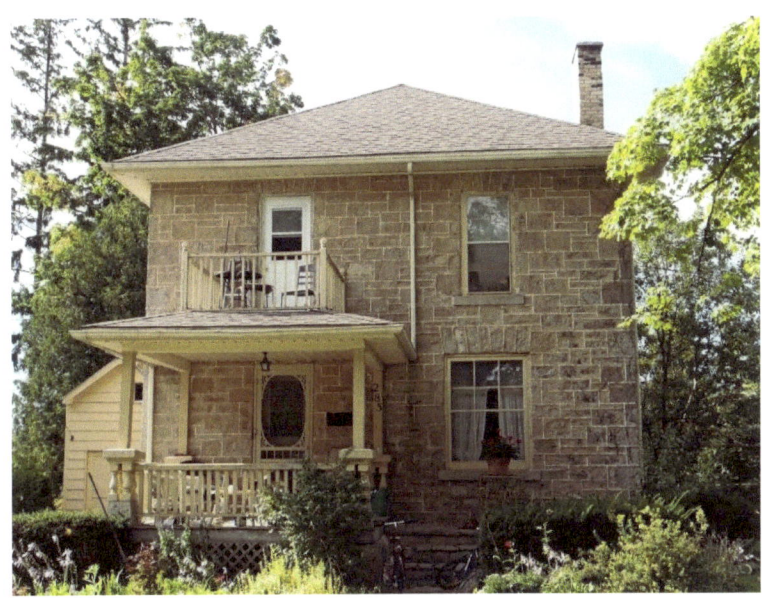

285 Union Street – hipped roof, second floor balcony

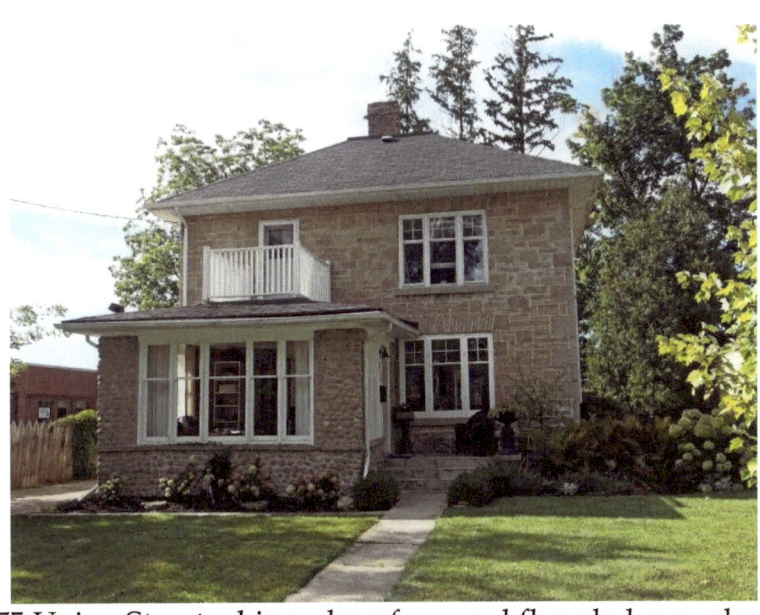

275 Union Street – hipped roof, second floor balcony above enclosed porch

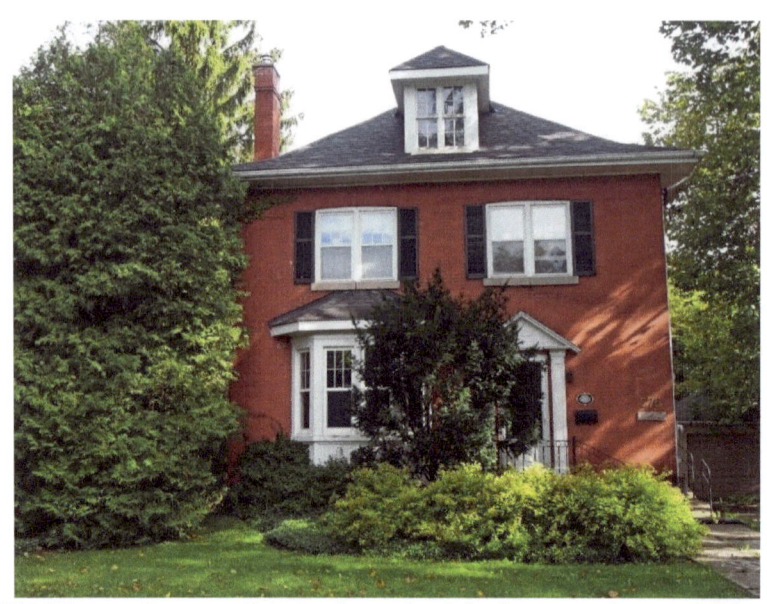

276 Union Street – hipped roof with dormer, bay window

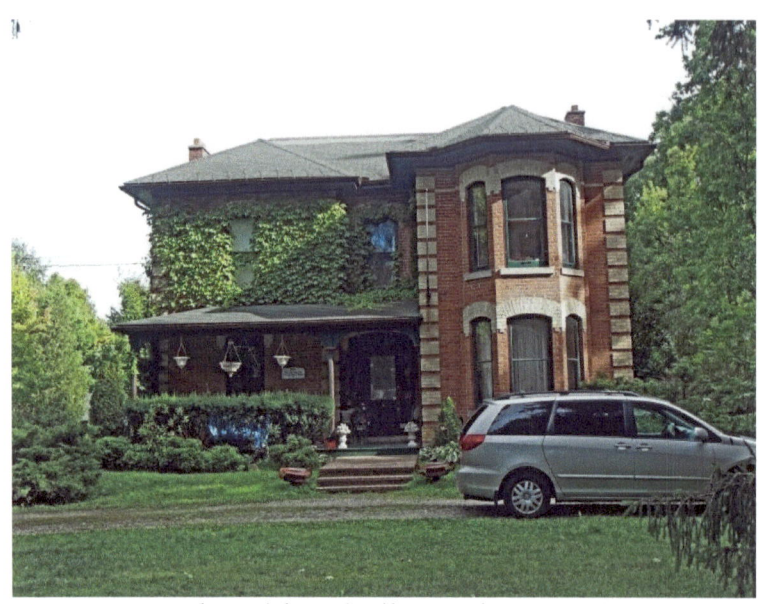

Union Street – The Old Melville Presbyterian Manse c. 1890
Dichromatic brickwork, two-storey bay window, hipped roof

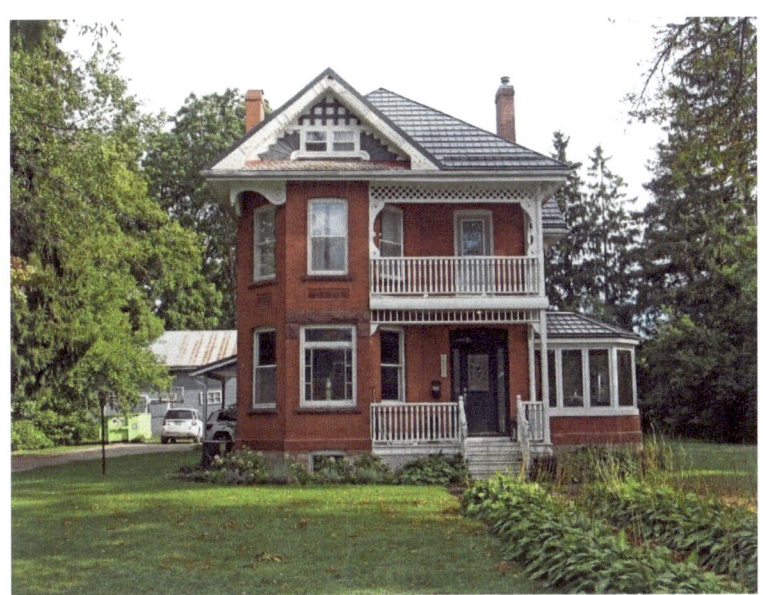

226 Union Street – Edwardian – second floor sleeping porch

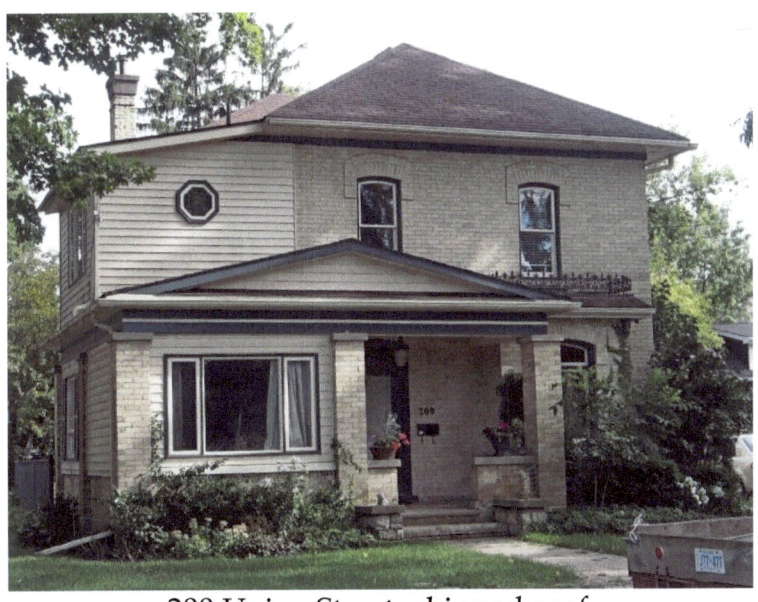

200 Union Street – hipped roof,
iron cresting above bay window

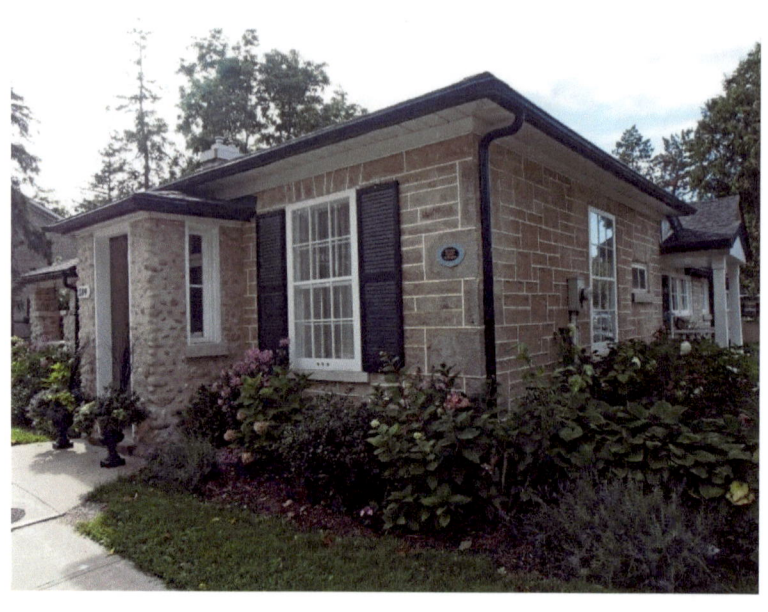

189 Union Street – Heritage Building – Regency Cottage –
hipped roof

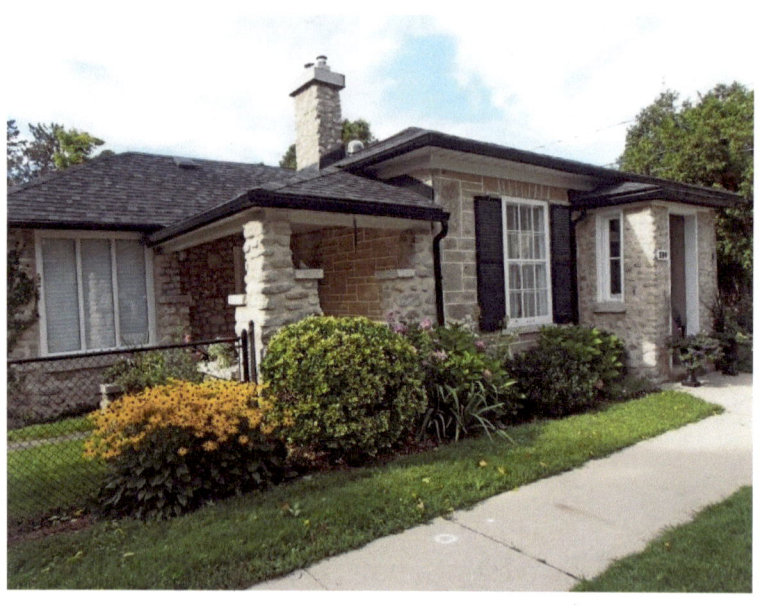

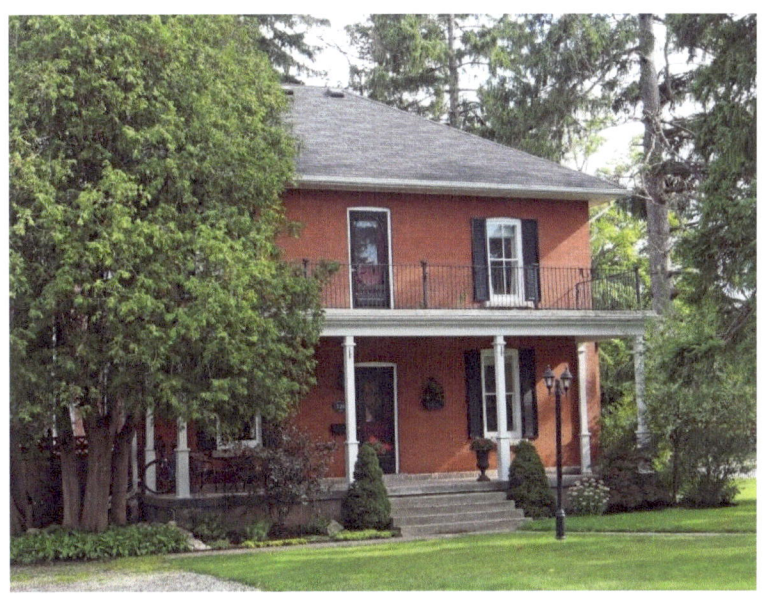

120 Union Street East – hipped roof, two-storey verandahs

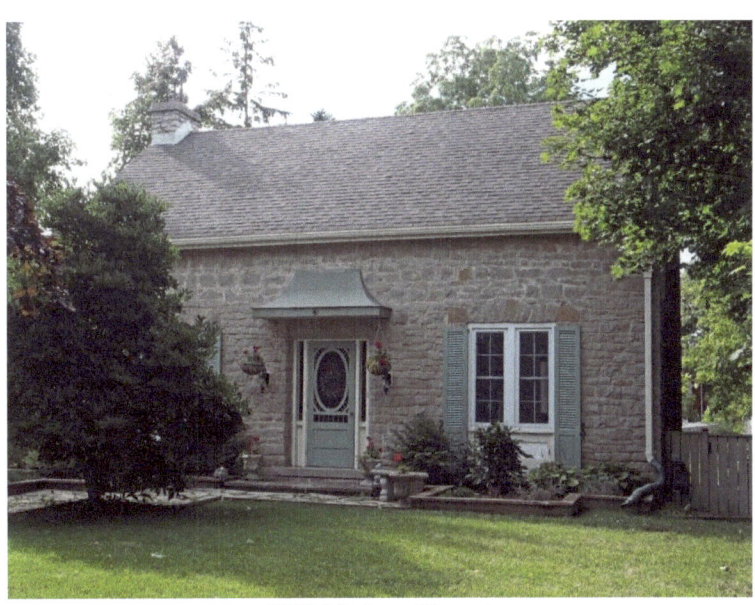

135 Union Street

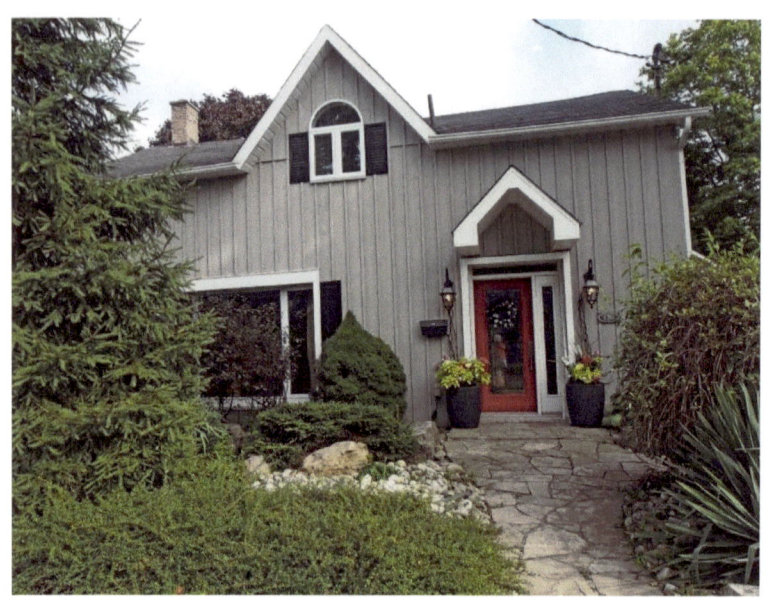

120 Union Street West – Gothic Cottage

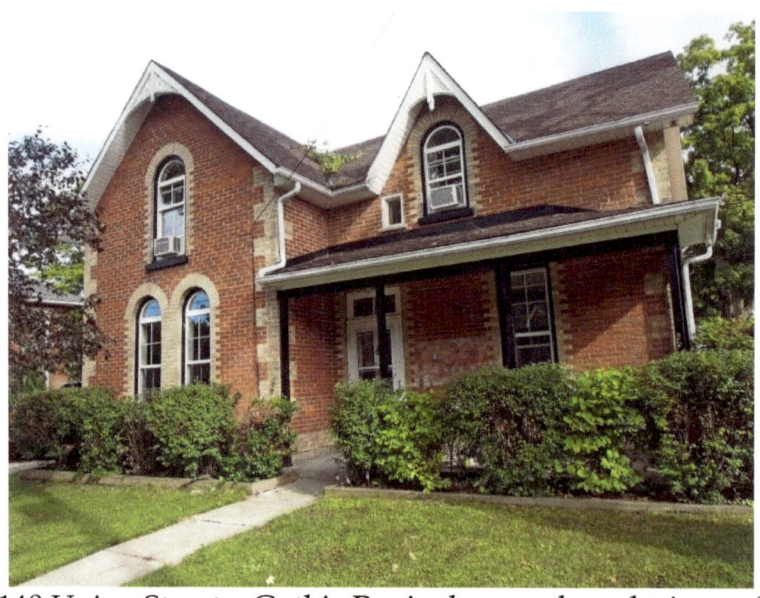

140 Union Street – Gothic Revival, verge board trim and finials on gables, corner quoins, dichromatic brickwork

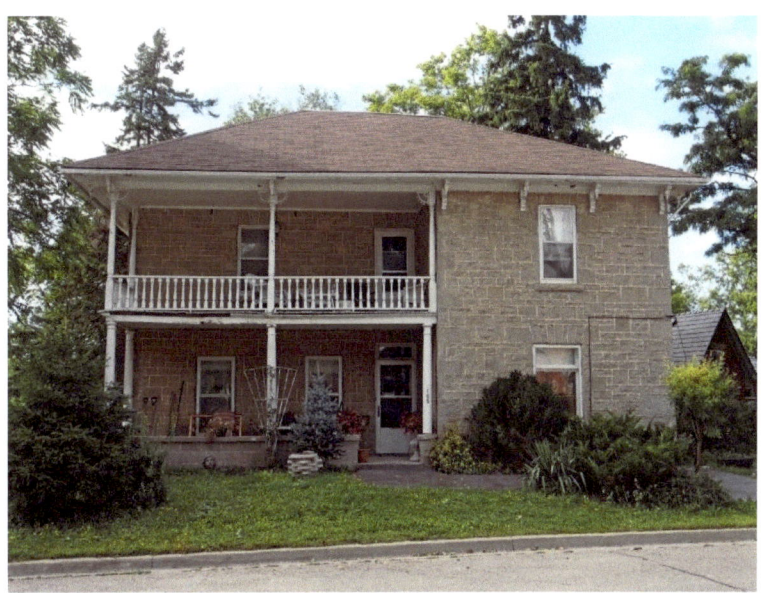

165 Union Street – two-storey verandah, hipped roof,
single cornice brackets

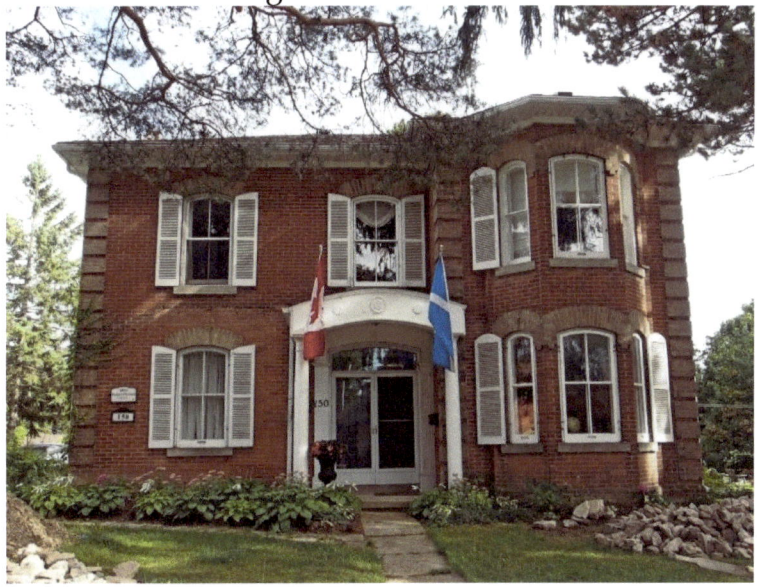

150 Union Street – Robert Phillips, Druggist c. 1883
Italianate, hipped roof, corner quoins,
two-storey tower-like bay

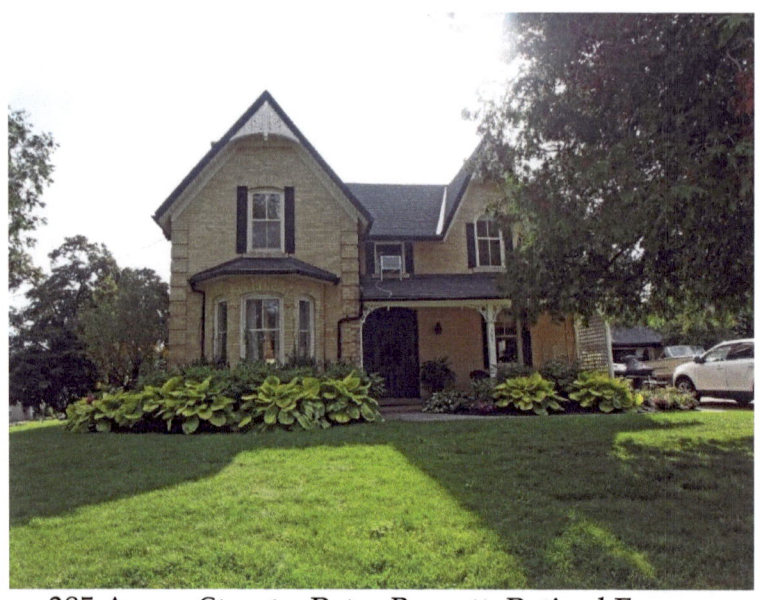

385 Angus Street – Peter Barnett, Retired Farmer
c. 1890 "Errolside" – Gothic Revival, verge board trim on gables, bay window

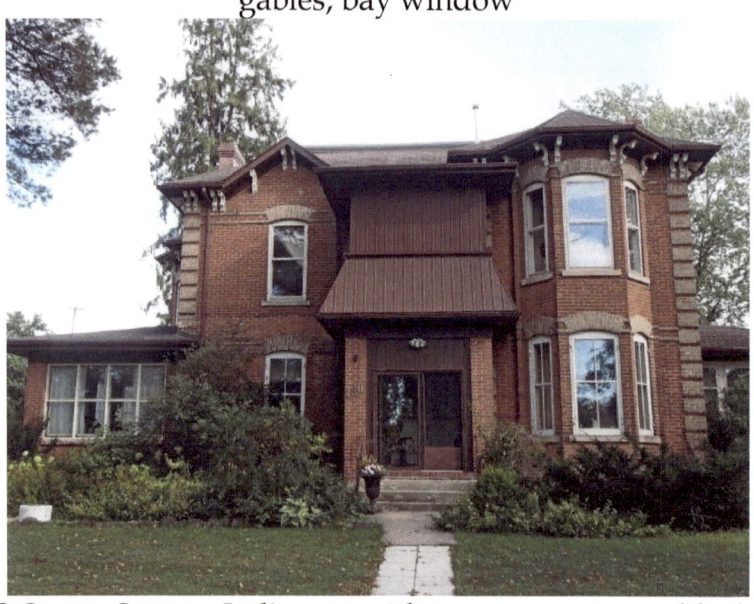

180 Queen Street – Italianate with two-storey tower-like bay, corner quoins, cornice brackets

Architectural Terms

Brackets: a decorative or weight-bearing structural element which forms a right angle with one side against a wall and the other under a projecting surface such as an eave or roof. Example: 180 Queen Street, Page 62	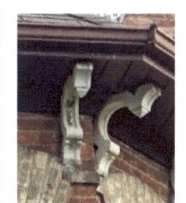
Cornice: originally the wooden overhang of the roof. With the use of stone, brick, iron and steel, the cornice is any projecting shelf at the top of a ceiling or roof. They can be very decorative. Example: #200, Page 26	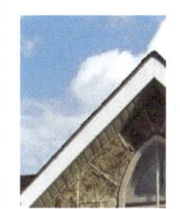
Cornice Return: decorative element on the end of a gable. Example: 141 St. Andrew Street, Page 27	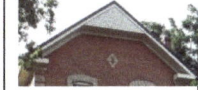
Decorative Brickwork Example: St. Andrew Street, Page 9	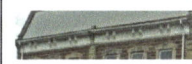
Dichromatic brickwork: the use of two colours of brick, tile or slate to decorate a façade. Example: 259 St. Andrew Street, Page 23	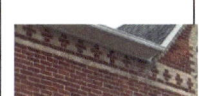
Dormer: (French for "sleep") a gable end window that pierces through the plane of a sloping roof surface to create usable space in the top floor or attic of a building by adding headroom. Example: 125 St. Andrew Street, Page 8	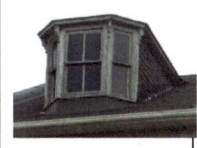

Gable: the triangular portion of a wall between the edges of a sloping roof. Example: 199 St. Patrick Street, Page 62	
Hipped Roof: a roof where all sides slope downwards to the walls with no gables. Example: 200 Union Street, Page 59	
Keystones and Voussoirs: a voussoir is a wedge-shaped element used in building an arch. A keystone is the central stone that locks all the stones into position, allowing the arch to bear weight. A keystone is often enlarged and embellished. Example: St. David Street, Page 31	
Lancet Window: a tall, narrow window with a pointed arch at its top. Example: 255 St. David Street, Page 30	
Mansard Roof: This style was popularized by Francois Mansart (1598-1666), an accomplished architect of the French Baroque period and especially fashionable during the Second French Empire (1852-1870). This roof is almost flat on the top section, with two slopes on each of its sides with the lower slope at a steeper angle than the upper and having dormer windows. Example: St. Andrew Street, downtown, Page 7	

Pediment: a triangular section above the horizontal structure (entablature), typically supported by columns. The inside of the triangle is called the tympanum. Example: 265 St. David's Street North, Page 32	
Quoin: masonry blocks at the corner of a wall, often a decorative feature, usually larger or of a different colour than the rest of the wall. Example: 141 St. Andrew Street, Page 27	
Rose Window: a circular window with ornamental tracery radiating from the centre. Example: 325 St. George Street West, St. Andrews Presbyterian Church, Page 47	
Verge board and Finial: also called bargeboards – hang from the projecting end of a roof and are often elaborately carved and ornamented. **Finial:** ornament added to the top of a gable, pinnacle, canopy or spire – a Gothic element. Example: 198 St. Andrew Street, Page 26	
Window Hood: A **hood** is the piece found above window openings, usually of an ornate design, and covers the top third of the opening. Hoods are commonly placed above arched or curved openings on both windows and doors. Example: downtown Fergus, Page 8	

Edwardian, 1900-1930 – This style bridges the ornate and elaborate styles of the Victorian era and the simplified styles of the 20th century. Balanced facades, simple roof lines, dormer windows, large front porches, and smooth brick surfaces are its characteristics. Example: 226 Union Street, Page 57	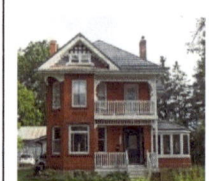
Georgian, before 1860 – This style began with the British King Georges in the 18th century. These buildings have balanced facades around a central door, medium-pitched gable roofs, and small paned windows. Example: St. David Street, Page 28	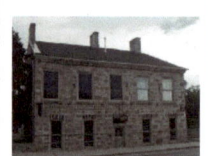
Gothic Revival, 1830-1890 – These decorative buildings have sharply-pitched gables with highly detailed verge boards, pointed-arch window openings, and dichromatic brickwork. It is a common style in Ontario. Example: 296 St. Andrew Street, Page 22	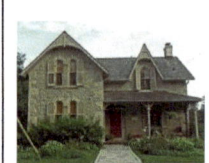
Italianate, 1850-1900 – It has wide-bracketed eaves, belvederes, wrap-around verandahs. Example: St. Andrew Street, Page 27	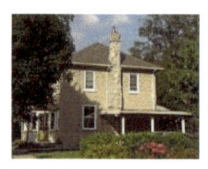

Neocolonial (also Colonial Revival, Georgian Revival or Neo-Georgian) architecture seeks to revive elements of architectural style of American colonial architecture of the period around the Revolutionary War which drew strongly from Georgian architecture of Great Britain. Architecture from the 18th and early 19th centuries in Ontario includes a wide assortment of detailing and ornament applied to a design centered around the fireplace and the source of water. Structures are typically two stories, have a symmetrical front facade with elaborate front doorways, often with decorative crown pediments, fanlights, and sidelights, symmetrical windows flanking the front entrance, often in pairs or threes, and columned porches. Example: 265 St. David Street North, Page 32	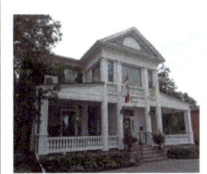
Regency Cottage, 1830-1860 – This style originated in England in 1815 and spread to Ontario later in the 19th century as British officers retired to Canada. It is a modest one-storey house with a low-pitched hip roof and has a symmetrical front façade. Example: St. Andrew Street, William Dass house, Page 24	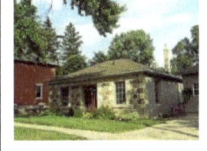

Second Empire, 1860-1880 – The mansard roof is the most noteworthy feature of this style and is evidence of the French origins. Projecting central towers and one or two-storey bays can also be present. Example: St. Andrew Street, Page 7	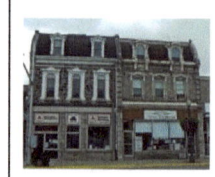
Tudor Revival – exposed timbers with stucco infill, multi-paned windows. Example: St. David Street, W. G. Beatty house, Page 33	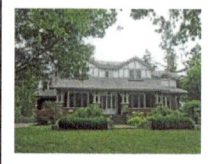